THE PLAYDATE

The Playdate

*Parents, Children, and the
New Expectations of Play*

Tamara R. Mose

NEW YORK UNIVERSITY PRESS

New York and London

NEW YORK UNIVERSITY PRESS
New York and London
www.nyupress.org

References to Internet websites (URLs) were accurate at the time of writing. Neither the author nor New York University Press is responsible for URLs that may have expired or changed since the manuscript was prepared.

ISBN: 978-0-8147-6051-2 (hardback)
ISBN: 978-0-4798-6629-8 (paperback)

For Library of Congress Cataloging-in-Publication data, please contact the Library of Congress.

New York University Press books are printed on acid-free paper, and their binding materials are chosen for strength and durability. We strive to use environmentally responsible suppliers and materials to the greatest extent possible in publishing our books.

Manufactured in the United States of America

10 9 8 7 6 5 4 3 2 1

Also available as an ebook

This book is dedicated to Alyssia, Matisse, and Tobias

CONTENTS

PREFACE

"Mommy! Can I pleeeeease have a playdate with Jack?" A playdate? I know what she means, but where did my five-year-old daughter get this language?

"Okay, but when and where?" I ask.

"At our house. I want him to see my house."

Jack's mother and I discuss the matter at pickup from kindergarten and decide that next week could work for both of us. She already has my e-mail address from the contact information, a list that was created at the beginning of the school year by the classroom parents who are in charge of communicating teacher requests. A few days later I receive an e-mail from Jack's mother suggesting possible dates and times for this "playdate." Arrangements are made.

A week later, on a Saturday, my daughter wakes up frantic to pick out her outfit for this "playdate." She is only five years old, but seems to have a sense of urgency, which she must get from me, about having company over to the house. She begins to clean her room. I don't even have to mention it to her. She makes up her bed and carefully places toys in a row against the back wall of her bedroom almost like a store display. Taking her cue, I become increasingly anxious and start cleaning the house. The playdate is about to begin.

Where did playdates come from? And what do they mean to parents who organize them? As a mother with small children and as a sociologist, I couldn't help but begin to ask myself these questions. My previous research on Caribbean nannies, who arrange playdates among the children in their care, increased my desire to delve deeper into the meaning of the playdate.[1] Once both of my children entered the public school system in Brooklyn, they were constantly being asked to have playdates with other children.[2] I understood the playdate to mean two or more children getting together so the kids could play, yet I did not have any previous context for the word since I hadn't grown up with "playdates" as part of my childhood. I realized I had been socialized to understand the meaning of the word through my communication with neighborhood friends, residents, and childcare providers in gentrified Brooklyn, where my family lives. I understood playdates to mean play for the children and a break for the parents or caregivers of children. Yet every time my daughter or son and I agreed to host or attend a "playdate" with neighborhood families, it rarely felt like a break; it was more like an effort to present ourselves as a decent black family or, during playdates with Caribbean childcare providers, as a decent West Indian family.[3]

After attending and hosting dozens of playdates and interviewing parents and teachers as part of my research about playdates, I began noticing the patterns of the playdate as an event. There was always preparation involved, whether preparing food for a private playdate at someone's home or packing a stroller for a playdate at a public park or zoo trip. Playdates seemed to follow a script, whereby parents and caregivers reprimanded children in a much lower tone than I would imagine in the private home, using the threat of having to leave the playdate for bad behavior, and having some intervention or activity on hand when two or more children began fighting or arguing, and it all ended with a tantrum or prolonged stream of tears when it was time to say good-bye and leave. The standard playdate blueprint also included more detailed nuances, nannies using playdates to combat the isolation they feel as domestic workers in the private sphere of someone else's home, and both nannies and parents separately using the opportunity to network among themselves for future employment.

I also began to notice that playdates tended to happen with people of the same social classes, races, and ethnicities. Nannies typically had playdates with other nannies of similar ethnic or racial background, and parents held playdates with other parents who were in similar socioeconomic situations. This is what intrigued me the most, and I questioned whether my initial observation was true. Were social classes meeting up only with one another, thereby reproducing or securing their own social class status? If so, how can this be, if the playdate is directed by a child in the first place (as many parents will have you believe), and this child has not perhaps quite grasped class and economic differences as completely as their adult caretakers? Also, what are the gender dynamics involved when initiating playdates? Did fathers have playdates with their children in the same way that mothers did?

In this book, I show how some parents include and exclude families through the playdate experience, thereby aligning themselves with like-minded parents who may further the social and life chances of their young children and themselves. Some parents reject playdates as something that "other types of parents" do. I also show how the playdate can help new parents sort through their new lives and responsibilities, from breastfeeding to simply caring for an infant who cannot actively interact through play. This book lays bare the logistics of organizing a playdate, how parents choose families to have playdates, why parents believe they have transitioned from simply having their children play down the street with neighbors to the more formally organized playdate, how playdates can begin as early as in infancy, and typically end toward middle school, and how children's birthday parties become a glamorized form of play-dates. In addition, I show how childcare providers have adopted the language of "the playdate" on behalf of their employers, thus reinforcing the class and cultural capital of children.

It is through the preparation for this book and many playdates that I came to appreciate the variety of ways we parent our children and per-haps think of them as somehow more fragile than our parents might have thought of us. Many questions arise. Are we serving our children or hindering them through the playdate? Are playdates something that only economically privileged people have in order to reproduce their class? Are working-class folks holding playdates in the same way as their more affluent counterparts? Do fathers and mothers engage in the playdate experience similarly? Do playdates reproduce gender norms by encouraging boys to play with boys and girls to play with girls in particular ways? In an age when instant technology is organizing our lives in almost every regard with the iPhone and other smartphones, is the playdate simply a by-product of having to schedule time for children to play with friends? While these are not questions that can be answered concisely, this book attempts to answer them through interviews with mothers, fathers, schoolteachers, and childcare providers from around New York City. The playdate experience is not only a New York phenomenon. We can track playdates in suburban areas and across the United States as well. However, New York offers a site where access to public transportation, perceptions of danger, and class, race, and ethnic diversity are so prevalent that the playdate has come to be negotiated in specific ways. It makes for a good case study as it epitomizes the international conversation about the social exclusion and social class reproduction that occur during the playdate. More importantly, it is a case study in how playdates are a widespread construction of twenty-first-century parenting and its anxieties about social class.

ACKNOWLEDGMENTS

This book would not see the light of day had it not been for the collaborative minds and actions of a variety of people. Typically family members are relegated to the end of the acknowledgments section of the book for fear that somehow placing them at the fore may make one's research look less rigorous. I'm not one for conformity and therefore choose to place them front and center. My children, now ages two, ten, and eleven, have served as great inspirations from the very beginning of this project by giving me insight into their social worlds. Alyssia and Matisse have given me the biggest challenge of my life, being a parent, and I have come to learn to be a better one because of them. Tobias will be the beneficiary of his siblings' teachings. This project would not be possible without Elaine Brown, who babysat my older children during a stay while I went from interview to interview across New York City. Thank you for your patience during this time. To my parents, Charmion and Kenrick Mose, who have also taken care of my children while I analyzed data and wrote the preliminary draft of this book in Canada, you have always been so selfless in helping me achieve my goals. I cannot thank you enough. Additional childcare has been given by my sister Debbie Mose and brother-in-law Norm Perreault, whom I am forever grateful to have in my life. And thanks to my sister Charonne Mose and my niece Kaaya Bufford for your continued support during my more chaotic moments in life.

To my editor over the last five years, Ilene Kalish, who saw this project as one that had potential to be a great contribution to how we understand parenting in urban centers. A mother herself, Ilene was able to play devil's advocate on several occasions to help foster a deeper and more objective analysis. I thank you for your support and belief in this book. Philip Kasinitz, I thank you for all of the lengthy discussions we had over this topic over the years as I began to write up the data for this book. Your insight provided me with a greater sense of how this book relates to the larger body of work on families. To the childcare providers I interviewed and observed for my first book, thank you once again for allowing me a window into your lives and for contributing yet again to another publication to shed light on how your work unfolds throughout the weekdays. To my colleagues Carolina Bank Muñoz and Gregory Smithsimon, I am indebted to you for all the time you took to read each chapter of this book in its preliminary stages and provide thoughtful comments throughout, sometimes to my chagrin. Your scholarly and practical knowledge helped to push the boundaries of how I engaged with the data. I could not have gotten through the exercise of writing another book without the complete support and devotion of my writing partner, fellow scholar, and friend Erynn Masi de Casanova. Erynn read through multiple drafts of this book at home, on planes, and at work. She has been my rock throughout the entire process. Words cannot express my gratitude to you. My two research assistants, Hagar Yazdiha and Erin Locks, I thank you for agreeing to help me with this project from interviewing participants to collecting literature at the library. Your dedication as graduate students will serve you well as future scholars. The blind reviewers for this book have given me ample notes and suggestions to make this a more robust piece of research. I thank you for taking the time to read the earlier versions of this manuscript and for giving of yourself and your time as an academic. I appreciate your candor and hope to know who you are one day. And to mon ami Dante' L. Wilson for supporting my academic efforts and being my greatest cheerleader as I entered the last phases of this project, during the most chaotic yet exhilarating year of my life. Your clarity and objectivity push me to be a better academic, friend, and mother. No mercy!

Last but not least, thank you to the parents whom I have interviewed for this project and to all the parents I have come to know through playdates. While some playdates followed the model of this book, "I rub your back and you rub mine," many turned into great friendships that I hope will last for years. It has been amazing hearing all of your stories and putting them together to express how anxieties about parenting come to be and how we manage them. Parenting is hard enough on its own, but when you add a dense urban center and a competitive, resource-rich culture to the mix, it can be even more daunting. We still have a lot of work to do, but at least we can now be more honest about what it is that we are doing.

Introduction

All the bathrooms are clean, dishes put away, beds made, floors Swiffered, laundry folded, garbage cans emptied, and toys put in their place and sorted for age appropriateness. The kitchen is full of aromas, boiling pasta, simmering sauce, freshly sliced carrots, celery, and oranges, all displayed on sparkling white plates. Lined up are juice boxes boasting their 100 percent organic label, plastic forks and plates, and beside them some half-folded white disposable napkins. On a solid black cutting board there is a perfect semicircle of whole-wheat and table water crackers, with three varieties of cheeses costing more than the outfit I am wearing. Some chilled mimosas sit in the fridge just in case, and fresh fruit, all prewashed and ready for consumption, on the dining room table in a large bowl next to the Annie's organic cheese crackers. Every minute pushes me to go over my list of things to do as the anticipation builds. Did they get lost on the way over? Did I give them the correct directions? Oh, I hope they don't cancel after I've prepared all of this food! The doorbell rings twice and the pitter-patter of little feet comes scurrying down the stairs as I reach the front door. I give my last warning to the kids to share all of their toys. I open the door and cheers and laughter fill the mudroom. I hug everyone entering and prepare for the ultimate social performance of—The Playdate.

This scene is typical of my five years of entertaining childcare providers, parents, and kids alike. Over time, my displays of extravagant entertainment have been modified as we have come to know the families for whom we once went all out. The playdate experience has become less about getting the kids together for social purposes and more about inviting those families we feel share our interests. For those living in Brooklyn, the settings for playdates include a public park among the dense residential neighborhoods of gentrified New York, and the private homes of residents in these neighborhoods as well as those living "out of zone." New York City has an educational system where children entering pre-kindergarten and kindergarten classes in the public school system must be zoned for the school they attend, meaning that they must live in the residential boundaries set by the New York Department of Education within specific districts. Children who are "out of zone" typically enter the schools because the families once lived "in zone" and have an older child attending the school. Some families become creative advocates for their children's education (which means that parents go to great lengths to deceive the system about their primary residence by obtaining water or electric bills from family or friends who are "in zone"). This is common practice in New York City since, as in other U.S. cities, the inequality in the school system is extreme. What emerge from these playdates are not only friendships that sometimes result in reciprocated free childcare, but more importantly, social and cultural capital for the parents involved.

Social capital, as conceived by the sociologist Pierre Bourdieu, who coined the term, refers to the number and types of people in one's network. By increasing one's network of interactions or contacts, one has the ability to gain or confer certain advantages to one's benefit or the benefit of those one knows. I argue in this book that playdates are planned events that parents organize to extend their network, thereby conferring advantages to their children as well as themselves, and that the playdate is not necessarily an event that is determined by the child.[1] Cultural capital, for Bourdieu, is gained through specific tastes in lifestyle or material goods (e.g., tastes in food, fashion, or education). This cultural capital may be gained through the attainment of certain social capital and other experiences. I will argue in this book not only that playdates are a way for parents to extend their network, but that they do so with middle- to upper-middle-class people who share certain middle- to upper-middle-class preferences in food, toy choices, and levels of education, all of which influence how parents and children navigate their social worlds.

This book takes the perspectives of parents, childcare providers, primary school teachers, and a children's studies college professor in New York City to understand the phenomenon of the playdate. I use the word "phenomenon" because the term "playdate" was not always used to describe children's play; however, it has now become the term for a common event that is used with a common understanding by those who participate. I define playdate as an arranged meeting, organized and supervised by parents or caregivers, between two or more children in order to play together at a specific time and place, for the most part at an indoor location. This book explains how parents think about the benefits or drawbacks of playdates. It also shows how participants view the tensions created by the media around the issue of child safety and how these tensions justify the creation of the playdate. More than anything, this book illustrates how parents and some teachers are able to reproduce social class. The goal of this book is to shed light on this practice in order to explore the social and cultural capital gained by members of middle- to upper-middle-class social groups, but also to show how certain groups of parents seek interaction with other adults through the playdate experience. This book therefore shows how playdates are critical social events for parents as well as children and how children's play should be taken seriously as a unit of analysis. It expands the existing literature on the reproduction of inequality while demonstrating the importance of how we manage our social worlds and the worlds of our children. This is important to understand because the playdate re-creates an elite social class despite the economic, ethnic, and racial diversity of an urban center.

This idea of studying playdates came to me one Sunday morning around 10:00 a.m., when my then husband and I decided to have our first "boy" playdate for our son. He mentioned two boys he was fond of, so we made plans with their parents to have them over for brunch one

Sunday. I became intrigued by their professions as we spoke, while the kids jumped off the bunk beds upstairs. One of the couples is a lawyer married to an artist, while the other is a screenwriter married to a man whom I later learned was the curator of the book lecture series at one of New York's public libraries. As I chatted with the curator and discussed my work as a sociologist who studied West Indian childcare providers, he asked me whether I knew the sociologist Philip Kasinitz. I said, "Yes, he was on my dissertation committee." He then said that he knew Phil really well and that I should give a talk at the library once my book was complete. It was at this moment that I started to realize how many times the parents I had invited to a playdate either knew someone I knew or offered to take family portraits for us, get us tickets to outings, or invite us to a trade show in which they participated. During this conversation with the curator, the idea of studying playdates became more concrete as I noticed that I was personally gaining social and cultural capital through the relationships I made as my son and daughter played with the other kids out of sight. I had been informally doing an ethnography of playdates for the past five years during my fieldwork on childcare providers and in my non-research life, but this topic seemed to demand further investigation.[2] Rather than subject my kids and others to staged playdates for the purposes of research, I came to study playdates using forty-one in-depth interviews conducted with a diverse group of parents and teachers and twenty-five interviews and ethnographic observations of Caribbean childcare providers across New York City. The aim was to determine how playdates acted as a means of gaining and reproducing social capital for certain classes of parents, how they are organized as a way of communicating exclusion, and how simple "play" turned into "playdates."[3]

Privatizing the Commons

The metaphor of the commons, a concept originating in sixteenth-century Britain land enclosures whereby the private enclosure of publicly held land and resources resulted in economic gain for particular groups of people, is highly applicable to a discussion of playdates.[4] The American ecologist Garrett Hardin discusses the effect of population growth on the global commons, where the personal choice to raise a family would strip away public resources and require "authoritarian regulatory population control."[5] Many authors have analyzed and deconstructed the commons as cultural (such as language or urban spaces), intellectual (patenting rights), or material (housing), with the same end result of commonly held capital being privatized for economic gain.[6] The playdate, I argue, is an example of this trend over the last two to three decades. In this book, the commons serves as a metaphor for the public sphere, where the goal of interaction is for the good of the whole population, children and parents alike. The commons might be neighborhood streets, local parks, or other playspaces. The enclosure of the commons is like a playdate that seeks to privatize space to preserve class reproduction, thereby obliterating the idea of a true "commons."

Playspaces may appear to be public commons since they are seen as spaces for shared social progress and practices. Playspaces are regulated by caregivers, parents, park personnel, and the like. However, the playdate is even more regulated as an enclosure to the common playspaces like public parks. Playdates are continuously subject to social control by some of the same regulators at the park, mainly parents or childcare providers, so that not only has children's play been enclosed, but as this book argues, it has also been commodified by parents in order to fulfill the acquired social and cultural capital gains expected of the middle- to upper-middle-class strata. By regulating and thereby commodifying the commons, parents may be undermining the socializing that more naturally occurs in the commons, or, for the purposes of this book, in parks, neighborhoods, or other public spaces. This turn inward, similar to that of historical suburbanization in the 1950s, when there was a retreat of people from city streets to their own backyards, changes social relations.[7] Once people retreated to their backyards, there was less interaction between classes and races and less inclusivity of people different from themselves. Boundaries became more defined. What is more surprising is that even in an urban environment such as New York, this turn inward and exclusivity can be observed today even though there is ample opportunity to be among others, given the close proximity to public spaces and dense housing.

This book uses the framework of the enclosed commons to understand how privatizing children's play has changed the interaction of both children and parents.

Parenting Children

Parenting can mean different things to different people. So too do the words "childhood" and "children." The first body of literature with which this book engages is that dealing with the commodification of childhood and parental reactions to societal constraints. Sharon Brookshaw, a museum studies professor, demonstrates the multiple meanings of childhood and children through her studies of museum content.[8] By examining museum artifacts and the archeological literature, she shows how meanings of childhood have changed from the prehistoric period to the twenty-first century throughout Britain and how ultimately childhood should be understood as a cultural construction. According to Brookshaw, museums tend not to display artifacts that deal with discipline, work, and health, reflecting how modern Western society has romanticized the meaning of childhood, and how parents want to protect children from the appearance of societal constraint. At the same time, her research shows how children become controlled by adults and society and turned into commodities as evidenced by the lack of homemade toys on display in British museums and an increase in mass-produced items such as books and clothing.[9] Children are placed in a material culture with purpose, meaning that adults have chosen the toys that ought to be displayed as a symbol of children's play and, in doing so, have not included the toys that children make out of scraps of material and play with, something that when all technology is taken away they still manage to create. This is similar to what occurs on playdates.

This book will show how parents can manipulate children's interactions in the playdate by carefully choosing the participants. The playdate becomes synonymous with "childhood" and consequently with the material conditions of childhood, which include specific objects, such as toys that define class status, and specific people who are allowed to interact with children of a certain class. In other words, in the same way that parents impose material objects such as toys purchased on behalf of their children that may signify to others a particular class stratum, they also impose playdates as a means of gaining cultural and social capital for themselves and their children and as a means to achieve homogeneity within an urban center.[10]

Multiple theories about childrearing, education, and the meaning of childhood inform the outlook of today's parents. Perhaps the earliest theory of child development is known as the Augustinian model, which suggests that children are innately wicked and vain, similar to what we see later in the twentieth-century novel *Lord of the Flies*, in which kids who are left to their own devices on an island beat and kill each other. This philosophy confirmed for parents that in order to save children from their own inherent "sin," adults should beat and corset them, and should protect themselves from children's bad behavior. This physical disciplinary approach lasted for centuries and continues today to some degree, though many view it very negatively.

Arguments against the Augustinian model were elaborated as early as the seventeenth and eighteenth centuries by John Locke and Jean-Jacques Rousseau. In his 1693 work *Some Thoughts Concerning Education*, Locke offers this critique: "Beating is the worst, and therefore the last means to be us'd in the correction of children, and that only in the cases of extremity, after all gently ways have been try'd, and proved unsuccessful; which, if well observ'd, there will very seldom be any need of blows" (section 81). Locke proposed that a child's mind is a blank slate (*tabula rasa*) that is affected solely by its environment. It is the child's environment and social interactions that will determine her or his behavioral outcomes or life chances. The child will reflect whatever it is that we put into him or her, and so Locke suggests that parents should raise their children to understand virtue and develop good habits through the process of education.

Rousseau, on the other hand, saw children as pure and good by nature. His theory suggests that children should be allowed to simply play, forget society, forget science, and develop naturally.[11] If a child intentionally breaks a cup, then she or he will learn that he or she will not be able to drink: "Give nature time to work before you take over her business, lest you interfere with her dealings. You assert that you know the value of time and are afraid to waste it. You fail to perceive that it is a greater waste of time to use it ill than to do nothing, and that a child ill taught is further from virtue than a child who has learnt nothing at all. You are afraid to see him spending his early years doing nothing. What! is it nothing to be happy, nothing to run and jump all day? He will never be so busy again all his life long."[12] Locke, however, would suggest that parents explain to the child why he or she shouldn't break the cup and then give the child a new cup. These two different philosophies have informed the study of childhood in both psychology and philosophy for centuries. These ideas permeate today's parenting magazines, leaving parents with opposing ideas of how to raise their children and asking themselves, "Do we allow children to explore freely and discover, or do we give them parameters through education to prevent failure?"

These opposing ideas are further analyzed by the sociologist Markella Rutherford. In her book *Adult Supervision Required*, Rutherford discusses how parenting magazines promote parenting ideals and philosophies, leaving families few options to choose from.[13] She also shows that when children do have a voice and autonomy in the household to make choices and decisions that affect their own lives, their autonomy is stunted by outside controls such as surveillance in the public sphere by other parents and authorities. On the one hand, children are expected to make independent decisions, but once they are confronted outside the home, this is all mediated by other adults. This book will show how mediation occurs not only outside the home, but inside the home as well in the case of the playdate.

Given such philosophies shaping how parents interact with their children, and given the idea that childhood is a commodity, the question of how children influence the economy began to take shape in the twentieth century as labor laws changed. The economic sociologist Viviana Zelizer shows that prior to the 1920s children were thought of as villainous if they were idle, and parents maintained childrearing practices that embodied the belief that children should work hard.[14] In her book *Pricing the Priceless Child*, Zelizer explains that it was not until the 1920s that child labor laws began reshaping the attitudes of parents, who over time came to see children as "priceless" and not capable of making a significant economic impact.[15] The new laws emphasized the "rights" of children, affecting how parents interacted with and raised them.

While other disciplines have delved into the psychological impact of parenting on children, there has been a significant body of sociological work that tends to be overlooked. In the 1970s, the sociologist and feminist scholar Alice Rossi discussed the biosocial effects of parenting by looking at how stress in a pregnant woman's body impacts a child's behavior after birth, how birth order acts as a determinant for parenting, and how childcare historically focused on women entering the workforce instead of the child's welfare. Rossi concludes that families living in close quarters would benefit from maintaining their traditional extended family structure, lowering maternal stress by having other "mothers" share in the responsibility of raising children. There is no discussion of how men are integrated in the raising of children, because as Rossi put it, "Men are rarely involved in the care of the very young. . . . The male is more apt to deal only with older children."[16] While this may have been true of the seventies and earlier decades, Rossi's theory does not hold true today. The present study shows how men are involved with their children today and how some of what Rossi states about mothers sharing in childrearing is reflected in playdates. In other work, Rossi discovers that men and women are less prepared for parenthood than they are for marriage and occupations. Parenthood thrusts them into dual roles that are not traditionally "male" (sole provider) or "female" (stay-at-home mom). She shows how parenthood occurs in developmental stages over time and how roles are negotiated and shared between men and women depending on the social climate. This book will argue that the twenty-first-century social climate, including heavy media coverage of crime, directly impacts how parents control the play of children while at the same time creating a social event for parents and children in the pursuit of reifying class status.[17]

While Rossi analyzed biosocial effects of parenthood, family sociologists Adrianne Frech and Rachel T. Kimbro look specifically at how the psychological well-being of mothers impacts parental behaviors, especially in low-income neighborhoods.[18] They show that "investing time in activities beneficial for children may increase mothers' self assessed parenting skills or self-esteem."[19] While these two authors discuss child activities such as playing at home alone or outdoors, they do not focus specifically on playdates. However, they do indicate that mothers' fears of neighborhood violence, more pronounced in low-income neighborhoods, lead them to let their children watch more television and play more video games, thus decreasing the mothers' ability to interact with neighbors and the children's interaction with others in the community. Frech and Kimbro conclude that there is a need for neighborhood intervention (quality neighbor interactions) to decrease depression among mothers in low-income neighborhoods and for parental interaction to become more positive. What they do not address fully, however, is that lower-income parents may have multiple jobs or work at odd hours, causing fatigue and preventing them from engaging fully with their children. Playdates, as outlined in this book, are viewed as an antidote to the fear of violence that is portrayed in the media according to the middle- to upper-middle-class families interviewed. Yet the seemingly forced separation from community that leads lower-income kids to watch television is seen as dysfunctional by their middle- and upper-middle-class counterparts. It is this control through the playdate that mediates how classes of people reproduce cultural and social capital.

Parents have control over children, but so too do social policies. In Britain, the sociologists Adrian James and Allison James show that policies affect how society views and shapes "childhood."[20] James and James argue that higher regulation of educational standards equates to more social control over children and that this new curricular intensification, while masked as a way to ameliorate the gaps between learning in school and at home, is simply another way of socially controlling children, particularly teenagers, in their out-of-school lives, including their socialization with peers. In Britain, police now have authority to stop children not in school during the schoolday (something that U.S. police have long done), parents are held accountable for what children do during school, and ultimately, James and James argue, children lack any agency under these new laws while they are increasingly being monitored and regulated. Though the authors admit that there are some benefits to the new policies, they maintain that adults ultimately shape how children are seen or not seen as citizens. Like government officials, parents believe that children are incapable of making good choices on their own. While many children in this book show some agency in "choosing" playdate partners, parents admit to shaping the choices their children make or simply dictating through action their children's choices. These choices are used to ensure that parents maintain social and cultural capital gains and promote their children's future because children are increasingly seen as only part of the culture of America and not as full citizens. A parent's control through the playdate is a reflection of the social institutions that children will learn to navigate on their own as well as a reflection of parental anxieties. Parents are massaging how children socialize by creating a commodified version of children's play through the playdate.[21] We can assume, then, that middle- to upper-middle-class parents have imposed a model of the playdate on children as a response to societal anxieties, including parents' anxieties about having to work long hours and therefore attempting to bridge the gap between school and home life.

Although policies can shape how children are monitored by society or by parents, so too can the spaces where children play. Holly Blackford, an English professor at Rutgers University, studied the panoptic effects of children playing in a park versus playing in McDonald's playspaces.[22] She noted how playgrounds are monitored by adults, mostly women, who occupy the benches at suburban parks in San Francisco. Children internalize that they are being watched even if they are not being seen in each transgression. She posits that children begin to self-monitor in this setting and surveillance is internalized, much like Foucault's theory of the Panopticon.[23] Foucault's concept of the Panopticon, which was originally theorized by Jeremy Bentham in the late eighteenth century, suggested that when inmates are visible from a central post that controls and monitors their behavior in order to implement discipline, the inmates eventually begin to monitor each other's behavior even when there is no authority figure in the central post. The inmates themselves become self-disciplined. Blackford noticed the opposite in commercial spaces, such as the ones in McDonald's. In commercial spaces, kids are not monitored in the same way as in the playground because there are tunnels that block the children from parents' vision. Parents tend to sit on the periphery socializing without constant monitoring and therefore, this type of play is more reflective of how working-class children played in the streets without supervision in the nineteenth and twentieth centuries.[24] Playing in the street in earlier times was sometimes synonymous with both danger (since children could get into trouble without adult supervision) and autonomy (since they could make up their own rules during play). In a commercial setting, kids appear to have more "free play" than in the playground, but it is also a site of consumption and control in that parental interaction is limited to how much food is eaten in the McDonald's playspace.[25] This type of interaction is perhaps why we see a proliferation of indoor spaces catering to children's play in New York City. Commercial spaces cater to the child's sense of freedom although they are entirely controlled, involving as they do the consumption of food and spending of money; many of the popular indoor spaces in New York cost a good sum and attract mostly middle- to upper-middle-class families or the caregivers who work on their behalf.

Consumption and control have thus impacted the parenting of children. But how have commercialism and merchandising impacted children and their families? The sociologist Alison Pugh's book *Longing and Belonging* looks at children in the Oakland area and how merchandising and consumerism give these children a sense that they deserve certain products, as well as a sense of belonging to a social group, or what she calls "economy of dignity."[26] She discusses how children "need" certain toys and if they do not have them they risk a sense of not belonging. Pugh talks about this shift from "wanting," or fulfilling desires, to an actual need, in which if your child does not have a portable game console, then she or he is not like everybody else and thus loses a sense of belonging. In order to maintain this belonging, you actually need these material things. However, she also argues that middle- and upper-middle-class parents become ambivalent about this consumption and attempt to restrain excessive consumer habits through the administration of allowances and specific rules about spending, although, as she points out, consumption eventually prevails. As one of my interviewees said, "If they [other children] have the Playskool [toy house] that costs $3,500, do I have to buy a Playskool so that my child has what other children have?" Longing and belonging were evident in the ways participants in my research discussed the idea of a playdate. Parents wanted to ensure that they were keeping up with other families in terms of the food they offer at a playdate or the types of birthday parties they throw for their child even if at first they downplayed its necessity. These various childrearing philosophies that parents have been socialized with, as well as the more contemporary literature of how children fit into a capitalistic model of consumption, subconsciously shape how parents begin their journey into parenthood. This book takes the playdate as an event in which these various meanings of childhood, parental anxieties, socially controlled "nature," and material conditions converge.

The second body of literature and theoretical framework deals with class reproduction and the inevitable exclusion that comes along with it. The sociologist Annette Lareau's analysis of class and race (in terms of preparing children as future citizens) uncovers how middle-class children, or what may be deemed "over-class" children (those with too many privileges), have a number of advantages, including a hyper-scheduled daily life, that confer specialized social skills that play out later in life. Other scholars have also shown how these hyper-scheduled lives ironically can be seen as a disadvantage for some families.[27] This structured life may include activities such as sports, music lessons, or scouting programs. This schedule is run very much like a business, often reflecting not only work positions of middle- to upper-middle-class jobs, but also how children and their parents plan rigidly scheduled leisure time. Some may call overscheduling an effect of the rationalization of modern society with its "emphasis on efficiency, predictability, control, and calculability."[28] Such scheduling of activities by middle- to upper-middle-class parents is done in order to confer advantages on their children in what Lareau calls "concerted cultivation," but since parents rarely know what skills their children will ultimately need in a rapidly changing economy, they tend to give their children broad experiences.[29] In this work, I will examine how playdates are not only a site for consumption, but also a product of social class reproduction that results in exclusion under structural conditions that allow parents to reify inequality among families.

Social Class Reproduction

Looking at parents' playdate participation, I was able to explain their interactions by using the concepts of social and cultural capital, terms originating in the social theory of Pierre Bourdieu and further elaborated by Alejandro Portes and other sociologists.[30] For the purposes of this book, social capital encompasses the potential resources stemming from intimate network relationships such as access to the skills of members of the group. Cultural capital is defined as the accumulation of education or other seemingly beneficial cultural knowledge.

Researchers in the United States already know that children's outcomes differ according to class as determined by socioeconomic status and that patterns reproduce themselves, so that the likelihood of associating with the class in which you grew up, or the neighboring one, is great. Class structure in the United States is stratified according to income level and typically divided into three categories: the working class, the middle class, and the upper-middle class. For this book, the *upper-middle class* would include those with a household income in excess of $70,000, but typically more than six figures, including inheritances, along with at least one partner with a college or postgraduate degree. Indirectly, then, children who are getting such skills as learning to play the piano and talking to adults like peers will have a payoff at some point in their lives. At the same time, researchers also know that because of the privileges that come with class membership, children from the upper-middle class are going to have those advantages anyway. Also, those without the middle-class networks and experiences may have similar success to those outside their class or economic grouping, so it is not an exact science in terms of mobility and continuity. However, for the most part, as Lareau has stated, class reproduction is real and we can see the differences in children's play: middle-class parents will pay for classes and more structured play, while the working-class and poor will have less structured activities, yet more creative play.[31] As the working-class and poor tend to their basic needs, making sure they have food and other life necessities, middle- and upper-middle-class parents are able to splurge on rearing their children by using extravagant resources that shape and reflect class views. It is important to note here that these resources are shaped by the very work situations of the parents themselves. Many of the middle- to upper-middle-class homes have a parent working in a white-collar profession. This can provide a wider field for more independent thinking than in working-class jobs, where there tend to be more directives with less opportunity for creativity. These "social chits" that the middle and upper-middle class are actively engaged in developing may be leveraged in the case of the playdate.[32]

Why New York?

Certainly New York is not the only city where playdates occur. It is, however, a dynamic urban center where the sheer density of its heterogeneous population and housing makes it an unparalleled site of analysis. In New York, more families are staying in the city or moving into the city to raise their children than are moving out to the suburbs. According to the 2010 census, there has been a steady increase of families moving to New York City from 2007 to 2010, more than the number moving out of New York. In addition, the census shows that households in Manhattan with children under the age of five as well as married couples with children are on the rise since 2000, making New York City an ideal site for the study of families and children's play.[33] The gentrification of New York and its boroughs, especially Brooklyn, allows for a better analysis of how families are cultivating their interests (whether familial or other) in an increasingly diverse but segregated city. As the sociologists John Mollenkopf and Manuel Castells stated in their book *Dual City*, New York has seen some of the most polarizing racial and income disparities, which contributed to the class tensions seen in the 1980s.[34] These tensions, alongside the increases in families and children and gentrification by the middle- and upper-middle-class and subsequent displacement of working-class residents, many of them blacks and Latinos, make New York a unique city to study, one central to understanding larger nationwide changes. Gentrification becomes relevant here, as it is spurred by typically white middle- and upper-middle-class groups and creates anxieties about class membership, since gentrifiers attempt to maintain their class privileges in terms of access to housing stock, amenities, and other resources. Those living in gentrified neighborhoods are hypersensitized to the changes that are constantly occurring to their housing values and want to ensure that their class status endures.

According to the 2013 edition of *The Newest New Yorkers*, New York City exhibits unique diversity. A large portion (one-third) of its foreign-born residents arrived after 2000, almost half of its population speaks a language other than English, and currently its "unmatched diversity epitomizes the world city."[35] What's more, there are far more small foreign-born groups, with Dominicans constituting the largest in the city, yet making up only 12 percent of the foreign-born. In 2011, "1.09 million immigrants lived in Queens while 946,500 lived in Brooklyn,"[36] making Brooklyn one of the most diverse places to live.

New York's outdoor spaces also create unique habitats for families diverse in race and class, and various ways to use such space. These spaces offer parents a variety of options in terms of play for children. Between the older public parks offering baseball, soccer fields, and sprinklers for water play, and destination parks that are now being built with modern elaborate climbing apparatuses such as Brooklyn Bridge Park at the end of Atlantic Avenue and Columbia Street in Brooklyn, caregivers have almost unlimited options for outdoor play. Public libraries, children's zoos, and botanical gardens also give refuge to caregivers with small children in all the boroughs. Some of these places, however, require access to transportation such as the subway or buses, and depending on where one lives, it can take over an hour to reach a destination (as in many cities).

New York businesses have also become quite creative with their play-date options for parents due to the small living quarters that most reside in. In affluent neighborhoods of New York, indoor play areas that mimic the types found in malls around the country are constantly being developed for toddlers and their caregivers, ranging in price from six dollars per hour of play to annual memberships of $1,200. These bounded spaces may double as a dance or gymnastics studio during certain hours, with time set aside for indoor recreational play offering padded areas for exploration with toys, books, and instruments. In Tribeca at the time of this study, the Moomah Café offered a one-hour playdate in its virtual green space room for sixty dollars.[37] Many cafés throughout Brooklyn now have a dedicated corner with children's books, games, and toys. New York also houses children's museums where kids can touch almost all items on exhibit, have lunch, and participate in daily entertainment. All of these indoor areas offer relief to caregivers on days when going to public parks is not an option due to weather conditions. These spaces also give caregivers a place to congregate and create community with one another while attempting to break some of the monotony of their active days.[38]

Even with all of these helpful resources, New York City, unlike some other major cities, epitomizes a fear of public spaces due to random crime reports and racialized fears that have permeated all city news cycles. Due to media portrayals, New York is seen as rough, chaotic, gritty, or some might say a scary place to live. There were racialized images of crime in New York from the 1960s that justified "white flight"; New York was highlighted as home to the Mafia in the 1970s, to drug addicts in the 1980s, to the extreme poor dispersed throughout, and to the housing project rappers of Brooklyn and Queens who make music about racism, violence toward black residents, and inequality.[39] This image is compounded by the high rates of crime that plagued New York for decades. Although the negative image stands in most people's minds, the truth of the matter is that crime in New York has been declining for two decades. Though a discussion of the law enforcement policies that have contributed to this decline is outside the scope of this work, I argue that the negative image is still prevalent in the media, including movies, newspapers, and television news.[40]

The old newspaper adage is true: "If it bleeds, it leads." Starting in the late 1970s with the kidnapping of six-year-old Etan Patz in Manhattan, and continuing throughout the 1980s, the media created a moral panic around child abductions, prompting the milk carton phenomenon, the placement of a missing child's photograph on the back of milk cartons

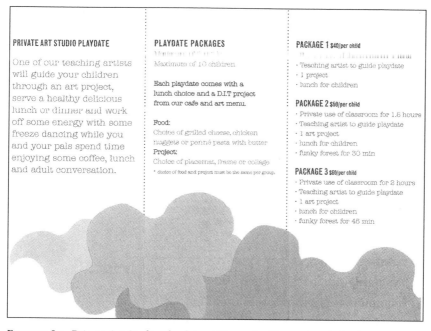

FIGURE I.1. Private Art Studio Playdate at Moomah offers a virtual playdate space (Funky Forest) for children, an art project, lunch, and artist-guided playdates.

to ensure maximum possibility of identification by the population. The cultivation effect, or long-term effect of media consumption, magnifies kidnappings (although many do go unreported) and glorifies prototypical characteristics.[41] This was evidenced further with the reopening of the Patz case in 2012, which reignited the public fear of kidnappings. For three decades, one child's kidnapping has defined New York's fear of letting children walk to a bus stop on their own, thus creating a moral panic. For other parts of the country, the prototypes do not end there. The media will generally lead with a young white girl with blonde hair from some safe suburb in the country who was kidnapped by a stranger without acknowledging that most kidnappings that are reported are carried out by parents, stepparents, and family friends.[42] We hear about the stereotypical case out of proportion to the actual threat. Even though the actual threat is statistically minimal, parents are left to wonder, "If these kidnappings could happen in a safe suburb, what is the chance that it could happen in a city that is stereotypically dangerous?" This moral panic, as considered later in the book, is discussed by almost every participant in my research as something that influences their decision to organize playdates, including parents who grew up in New York and those who did not.[43]

More than all of this, New York has a higher concentration of diversity (economic, racial, and ethnic) and, as C. Wright Mills terms it, of the power elite (financiers, corporations, those with institutional power) who determine the economic course the rest of the nation takes, which makes New York unique. There are limitations to this study due to this concentration of diversity and institutional power in that it is not representative of the rest of the country. Therefore, it is important to understand these limitations with regard to generalizability across various states.

Its rich history, media image of violence, array of outdoor and indoor spaces, and unique diversity and concentrated institutional influence suggest that New York is a prime city in which to study the playdate phenomenon and to study how families are reconstructing their children's play as a reaction to media sensationalism and other social forces.

Methods

For this book, I conducted forty-one semi-structured interviews from June 2010 to August 2011. There were thirty-four women and seven men, of whom four were in their twenties, nineteen in their thirties, fifteen in their forties, two in their fifties, and one in her sixties. From this group, there were thirteen people of color, including three who self-identified as black or West Indian, five as Asian, and five as Hispanic/Latino. Five white participants self-identified as Jewish (not white), while the remaining twenty-three white interviewees identified as Caucasian, mixed, white, or European. All interviewees except two had children. Of those who did have children, there were between one and four children in the family, ranging in age from six months to twenty-eight years old. Annual income ranged from $20,000 to $500,000. All participants lived in the New York City area, with twenty living in Brooklyn, seventeen in Manhattan, three on Long Island, and one in Queens. I specifically included Long Island since many of the homes in that area are spread farther apart than the other areas. I thought this might provide some contrast in terms of geographical constraints in hosting playdates. Participants ranged in occupation from financial consultant, graduate student, and marketing researcher to self-employed entrepreneur, yoga instructor, realtor, or stay-at-home parent. Included among the participants were three people who worked as private childcare center directors, two who worked as teachers and organizers of a playdate website, one who worked as a children's studies professor at a public university, and one who worked as a charter school administrator. Each interview lasted anywhere between one and three hours. All names in the book, except those of the organizers of the website, are pseudonyms to ensure the confidentiality of each participant.

Initial participants were recruited using convenience sampling from parents I came to know at my children's school. While this accounted for only three of the interviewees, the other participants were recruited to the project through snowball sampling. One of the parents I knew worked for a children's product line and used social media to place my recruitment ad. It was from this source that I began snowball sampling. In addition, my research assistant, who interviewed ten participants, worked at a charter school in Manhattan and was able to use snowball sampling through the parents whose children attended the school. Her recruitment accounted for nine of the participants. While this book includes interviews conducted by the two of us, our data showed significant overlap and well-defined patterns, allowing me to posit conclusive arguments.

After most interviews (except those of interviewees without children), I was asked whether I had children, and I found that as I divulged information about my family and children, this almost always resulted in more participant referrals. There seemed to be comfort for some interviewees in knowing that a parent was conducting the research and that I had a vested interest in the subject matter beyond simple research. Perhaps this humanized me in ways that suggested empathy or an understanding of childrearing. This perceived comfort at the end of most interviews could have been a result of my shared class or status level with many of the parents interviewed, since many were professionals. Those in working-class positions found ways to connect with me since we sometimes shared racial minority status. However, I believe that more often than not, any rapport at the end of the interview was due to our shared parenthood status. I occupied an insider status that my research assistant did not simply because I had children; however, this did not impact the data, only my ability to acquire more referrals at the conclusion of the interviews. It should be noted here that I did not bring my children to any of the interviews, and only two participants were interviewed with their children in the household. As Lareau and others have noted in their studies, most participants eventually fall into their everyday routine despite the interaction with researchers in private spaces. However, an interview-based method makes it challenging for participants to truly feel comfortable to the same degree as when a researcher becomes a constant presence in their life, as ethnographers do. For this reason, I found that it was key to connect with participants by divulging that I was a parent and earning their trust in a timely manner so that they would feel comfortable discussing the private intricacies of their children's play that go beyond the superficial, which they tended to elaborate on after they answered the interview questions.

While this method of research significantly departs from my previous work in ethnographic participant observation, this project captures the detail necessary to fully understand the playdate as a phenomenon. I used my previous interviews about playdates and ethnographic observations at playdates with twenty-five Caribbean childcare providers from 2004 to 2007 to understand the experiences of these women in their work on behalf of their employers. These providers were aged twenty-five to sixty-one and came from the countries of Grenada, Trinidad, Guyana, St. Lucia, St. Vincent, Jamaica, and Barbados. Their incomes ranged from $200 to $700 per week, but were not necessarily consistent, since these women labored in a precarious workforce with high turnover. I wanted to compare their experiences to those of the employers of childcare providers to answer questions such as, "How does it feel to have a playdate organized on your behalf?" or "How does the word 'play date' become adopted by cultures that never used the term?" I use my personal playdate experiences as a parent sparingly to further illustrate how people interact throughout the playdate experience and to detail how complicated the whole ordeal can become.

To initiate this study, my assistant and I contacted participants and interviewed them individually in a location of their choice. Only two participants asked to be interviewed together with someone else, one with her spouse and the second with her coworker. We met at the homes of participants, in local public parks, at workplaces (including corporate offices and schools), as well as restaurants. Participants were first given a short survey to provide demographic information such as their educational attainment, household salary, and family structure. They were then asked general questions about their experiences raising children in New York and their own personal recollection of how they were raised in their hometown. Specific questions regarding playdates followed. It was important for me to understand how participants defined a playdate, how frequently they had them, what activities were involved, and what type of meaning was derived from the playdate experience. I also asked questions that targeted participants' understanding of space (public and private), who was included or excluded from a playdate, and how the playdate was initiated. Lastly, in an effort to understand how playdates and birthday parties (hyper-playdates) contribute to community and society, I asked questions pertaining to job opportunities and networking as well as the extravagant nature of some birthday parties. While not an exhaustive account, these surveys and interviews helped to tell part of the story of what it means to New York City parents to have their children participate in playdates.

Plan of the Book

This book begins by detailing the moral panic surrounding child safety ("stranger danger") and how parents view their role as facilitators of their child's play practices. Parents discuss this moral panic as disseminated through the media as one of the reasons they prefer to organize "playdates" rather than allow their children to go out to "play," a distinction that parents are able to define.

The first chapter also looks at the playdate as a result of busy urban lives, in which parents are either working odd hours or expected to move at warp speed throughout the day, leaving only a tiny window of opportunity for the socialization of children. This chapter will describe how middle- to upper-middle-class parents use playdates to socialize their children into play in order to avoid perceived city dangers. The playdate essentially becomes framed as a date or a courting of other parents and their children.

Chapter 2 explains the logistics governing playdates, including where to have one, how many children will be invited, whether it is to be a drop-off playdate (in which parents do not participate), and what time of day is ideal. This chapter uncovers how even among affluent participants, certain playdates are avoided because they demand too much effort to execute.

Chapter 3 reveals which parents and children are excluded or included in the playdate experience. Full-time working parents appear to have less opportunity to immerse themselves in playdates and are therefore excluded by other parents due to their employment. The issue of the nanny's involvement in playdates and who organizes the playdate is also discussed here. Chapter 3 also examines playdates as a predominantly white, upper-middle-class phenomenon. Some mothers of color whom I interviewed feel that playdates are "a white people thing" that is used to exclude them from being members of this leisure class. Also in this chapter, parents discuss how playdates have contributed to their sense of community and even their sanity. Some began their playdate experiences as early as their child's first week of life. Through previously organized "mommy groups" that were initiated by their doula (one who aids in a natural childbirth), obstetrician/gynecologist, or pediatrician, women were able to find a support system where they could share resources, ideas about parenting, or a simple glass of wine to take the edge off during days filled with diaper changes, feedings, and other household duties. These mothers yearned for adult interaction in their newly formed parenting world. Often, employed women were left out of these circles once they returned to the workplace, and thus further exclusions were made. This chapter shows how social and cultural capital are transferred from the parent to the child, either implicitly or explicitly, through the construction of a playdate with "people like them" and how this continues the cycle of class reproduction.

Chapter 4 takes a pragmatic approach to the question of playdates and how they are organized. Food for the children was an essential element in the playdate experience for most of the interviewees. If parents were present at the playdate, wine, other beverages, and some snack would be expected as well. Along with food, discipline was expected to conform to the standards of modern parenting (i.e., no physical discipline). A parent's performance of "proper" discipline could also be seen as a marker of whether their family would be included in a repeat playdate and to gauge the success of playdates.

Finally, chapter 5 looks at birthday parties as hyper-playdates. While some see birthday parties as a private celebration for family and intimate friends, others discuss how one family can raise the bar of what is expected within an entire group of parents with an ostentatious birthday party. Pressure to ante up on what most would consider a modestly important occasion drives parents to impress others and ultimately establish a social circle of "people like us."

Together, these chapters will help scholars and parents think about how children's play has been redefined in recent years through the privatization of play. *The Playdate* will serve as a window into the reproduction of inequality while also shedding light on how parents are tasked with the complex job of raising decent citizens in a seemingly unpredictable urban environment.

1

From Play to Playdate

Moral Panic and Play Redefined

Within five minutes of a child abduction, an Amber Alert arrives on your cell phone, while at the same time, the television program you were watching segues from a missing child to one about a rampant school shooting. Remember when we used to see the photos of missing kids on the backs of milk cartons in the 1980s? Is the Amber Alert system, in which all radio and television stations and digital street signs alert the masses that a child has been recently abducted, better than the milk carton strategy? I sure hope so. Going from missing child immediately to children being shot by a disgruntled schoolmate or community member is enough to put anyone on high alert. I go through every day with such care to make sure that my children don't end up in one of those two (and other) situations, but I cannot control every aspect of their lives (or mine, for that matter). It is scary to think that at any turn, something tragic could happen to our children and that we have limited control over the matter. How can we find peace of mind in such volatile times?

This chapter will look at why parents arrange playdates for their children; how parents describe their perceptions about safety in public spaces; and how they perceive lack of green spaces, need for community, and issues dealing with scheduling, all of which ultimately leads to the redefinition of play in private spaces to reproduce social and cultural capital.

Today's parents are bombarded by media images that create concern for their child's safety.[1] Crystal is a forty-one-year-old self-identified European American mother who grew up in a suburb in the Midwest, but now lives in the Tribeca neighborhood of Manhattan. Her large modern loft sits near Ground Zero, the former site of the World Trade Center. She discussed her fears when asked about raising a child in New York and how her first-grade daughter plays. She was interviewed during a playdate in which her daughter moved back and forth between Crystal's loft and a neighbor's loft. Crystal explained, "They're exposed to a lot more adult-content imagery and language. Especially, you know, riding on the subways. She has a lot more questions than I ever had at her age. She can read, so you know, the subway ads, everything is a problem, . . . but I just always try to look at it as an opportunity . . . for conversation or discussions." She added, "I think in New York . . . the kids can't walk outside the building on their own." She went on to state that, in general, scheduling playdates and ensuring safety (safety from vulgar imagery) are her primary concerns because of the way children are unprotected from adult-content promotional material.

Many parents discussed the violent advertisements they saw when taking their children through the city subways and the types of commercials that are shown on television even on the children's programs. Just as Margaret Nelson found in her book about parents who constantly monitor their children in our hectic modern world, violence and sexually explicit images on television or in advertising created anxiety among parents of the middle to upper-middle class. Parents in this book revealed that after repeated exposure to such imagery, they felt that their fears were justified, thus creating a moral panic as a result of the relentlessly publicized violence against children.[2] A moral panic has been defined as the widespread public awareness of a type of crime that is repeatedly publicized. Through such publicity the image is created of a group of violent people who threaten the welfare and values of a society, and this image creates a public moral panic. In addition, fear is spread when violence is random but highly publicized, as in the kidnapping of Etan Patz in New York.[3]

Others expressed similar feelings about New York. Maria, a thirty-five-year-old Upper East Side Jewish mother who is raising two small children (ages five years and six months) across from Central Park, stated that while New York has greater resources and more classes for kids to participate in, there is less green space than other cities. The noise, dirtiness, and the general safety concerns for children, from what she saw in the news, were problems for her as a parent. Carol is a forty-three-year-old black British immigrant to New York who used to work as a psychological therapist in England (at the time of her interview she was unemployed), and is raising her kindergartener in Brooklyn. After only a few months in Brooklyn, her perspective on raising children already differed from the perspective she held in her native England. Carol had recently been part of a parenting cooperative where parents take turns caring for each other's children so the other parents could go out to dinner or on some other outing. Her experiences were different than in England, where she had a family network to rely on for her childcare needs. In New York she was still navigating the resources available to her. Carol's biggest issue to date with New York was simply trying to immerse herself in the culture, which she said was difficult because one did not know whom to trust, something she had learned through watching American television. Carol determined that organizing and participating in playdates would allow her to figure out whom she could trust in New York with her child.

Words such as "trust," "noise," and "caution" were used consistently by parents and fit with the popular perception of the negative realities of raising children in New York. They have been influenced to believe, whether consciously or subconsciously, through the media, that New York City is unsafe and full of dangerous people. Parents described their sense that bad people are lurking at every corner and therefore one ought not to get too close to anyone, no matter how nice they may seem. Participants in this book described how they always teach their children to be kind to people, but wary of their intentions. In her book *Adult Supervision Required*, Markella Rutherford discusses how parents' fears are perpetuated by the absence of children on neighborhood streets, which in turn drives parents to want their children indoors and away from adults who may be untrustworthy or dangerous.[4] If there are no children on the streets, there are no "eyes on the street," to borrow a term from the author and activist Jane Jacobs.[5] The other concern is that because of noise due to traffic and the lack of green space (despite New York's efforts to create more green spaces through its tree planting efforts and greenways), one may not be able to raise children in an environment conducive to learning or development. Although Maria lived directly across from one of the largest green spaces in the city, Central Park, New York's lack of ample green spaces was of concern to her should she venture out beyond her own neighborhood. While New York City has several green spaces (although one could contest that definition), people experience New York as a "concrete jungle." Green spaces, meaning parks with large trees and grass, are not equally distributed by race and class for the most part in New York City, and since urban green space is more concentrated, such as with Central Park, it affects how people experience a city in contrast to the way they experience a suburb.[6]

The other issue discussed by participants is a wish to feel connected to community. Carmen, a mother of one daughter, said, "Raising my daughter in New York is challenging and a little lonely despite the fact that there are so many people around. I find it hard to connect as a mother here in New York." While she also stated that this could be because she was a single mother, she said that she found it hard to relax because the city was so busy, and it became difficult for her to move around.[7] The sheer density of the city made her feel like a "stranger."[8] Despite the poor quality of the education offered in her small Massachusetts town in the 1980s, a town that also struggled with drugs and high unemployment after she left, it had once been prosperous and there was a strong Portuguese-speaking community that made her feel connected. She has yet to find that type of community in her area of Carroll Gardens (Brooklyn), where she rents an apartment with a roommate and works as a yoga instructor, earning a working-class wage of $32,000 a year. Sook, a forty-four-year-old Chinese American mother living in Brooklyn with her four children (all under the age of ten) and working full-time as a financial advisor on Wall Street, said that what she likes about New York are the "culturally diverse institutions." Sook's complaints are mostly related to the cost of living in Brooklyn (she owns a brownstone that costs a lot to maintain, since it is over a hundred years old) and her concern about the public school system and making sure that the schools are safe. Again, the safety issue came up in the interview, yet there was no concrete evidence that she could provide to suggest that the schools were unsafe other than the fact that there were security guards at the front desk of the school where her children attended. She was unfamiliar with the schools in Brooklyn before her children began attending, so this unfamiliarity grew into a fear for the safety of her children, a natural takeaway if you watch the news on any given day: schools are not safe for children, especially with bullying on the rise, according to Sook and other participants.

The news and schools now pay more attention to school bullying, as well as school shootings. Schools even participate in regular lockdown drills in order to prepare students and staff for any potential shooting threats. This, in concert with the unfamiliarity of Brooklyn schools, perpetuates Sook's fears in particular. Sook grew up in Chinatown and admits that she did not veer too far from there as a child; her opportunities were limited since her parents both worked full-time with minimal earnings. She said that, as one of five children, she was a latchkey kid and would walk home by herself and let herself into the home at a very young age, something she wouldn't have her kids do today, due to the perceived lack of safety in New York according to the news, and admittedly due to the fact that there are almost no children on the streets doing the same. It is this perceived lack of safety that creates fear and ultimately leads parents to find alternatives for their children to socialize in controlled environments such as the playdate.

All of these mothers, and other parents whom I interviewed, discussed issues of safety, especially the dangers to children portrayed on television newscasts, including school security and the safety of children who go home alone or simply go outside by themselves. As a response to this safety issue, parents were more inclined to organize playdates. As Laura, a twenty-seven-year-old African American mother of a first grader, stated, "The city is a rough place for people to have kids." She wanted to make sure that her child was in a controlled environment that would protect her from the reality that is New York City. The over-stimulation of advertisements for horror movies or sexualized content in subway ads and around the city makes some parents anxious about protecting their children from violent imagery.[9] On top of it all, there was a sense of disconnect for some who had yet to find their place in New York as residents and parents, mostly for those who did not grow up in New York and only had media images to draw on.

One mother, Jodi, however, clearly saw the inherent contradiction in what most mothers believe. Jodi grew up mostly in Brooklyn, but moved a lot as a child because she traveled with her father, who was a journalist and editor of a newspaper. She had traveled the world by the time she was her daughter's age (six). Jodi stated that "parenting maga-zines say raising children has changed because everybody is oversched-uled and parents are taking charge of their kids' social life in a different way." Parents, she noted, "are more concerned about safety, pedophiles, and somebody kidnapping your child, and this might not even be true. Mostly, things aren't really any less safe than twenty or thirty years ago. My husband has a book that says most of these fears are not based on real things, so you can let your child walk down the block, but who's going to do it? Nobody, because no one else does it. I think our parents were more involved in keeping us safe than people remember." Jodi was expressing a real concern as she talked about overscheduling (a real issue that parents in this book acknowledge), a matter to be taken up in more detail in a later chapter, and how this related to safety. In her discus-sion of overscheduling and its effects on parenting styles, Jodi is hinting at the differences in how women and men are socialized to fear public spaces. The overscheduling, coupled with this gender-based socializa-tion, attempts not only to create a child with certain skills, but also to avoid risk. Jodi suggested that by organizing playdates, parents feel that there is less opportunity for something bad to happen to their children.

Women are taught to fear outdoor spaces, what the geographer Gill Valentine called a "geography of fear."[10] In addition, women have been socialized to accept the private sphere of the home as a safe space that is contrasted to the public sphere, where they are or may be subject to harassment and violence.[11] In taking charge as a mother by overscheduling a child, one is attempting to ensure that the child is accounted for at all times and not roaming unsafe public spaces. That being said, this also relates to women working outside the home and having less time to account for their children's whereabouts. Women working outside the home want to ensure the safety of their children by enclosing them in private spaces that are considered safer, hence the enclosed commons of the playdate. Fathers in this study were not typically responsible for the children's schedules, so this was all directed by mothers even when fathers were the primary caregiver. Therefore, if one is a "good parent," one would have a heightened response to one's children's needs by ensuring that the child is active in all ways, but safely occupying indoor (read private) spaces. And thus the moral panic continues. Jodi's clarity on the media's role in the paranoia that pervades parenting in New York helps make clear how parents view New York as a city in which to raise children.[12]

New York City has long been seen as fraught with scandal and danger. In the summer of 2011, headlines featured the story of an eight-year-old Orthodox Jewish boy from Borough Park, Brooklyn, who was dismembered and stored in a man's fridge after the boy attempted to walk home by himself for the first time with his parents' approval. It was stated in the news that the man who committed the crime was from the same Orthodox community as the parents, and the motive for such a heinous crime was unclear. While it is important to be aware of this type of coverage, especially if the criminal has not been caught, it is of the sort that frightens parents into believing that their child could fall victim to such a kidnapping and what appeared to be a random murder by someone with a history of mental illness. It only takes one story such as this, covered over and over on television news, on the Internet, and in newspapers, for a viewer/reader to determine that this could be anyone's fate. Add to this the policing of parents by race and class, and the panic becomes even more pronounced. For example, the black South Carolina mother who was arrested for leaving her nine-year-old daughter at a nearby park while she worked at McDonald's due to lack of affordable childcare sparked debate about how young is too young for independence and whether the child was safe at a park on her own. Unlike this mother, the Jewish parents of the boy who was murdered were never arrested. Yes, these are two very different states, yet the stories beg the question. How do we judge good versus bad parenting, what are the anxieties associated with parenting, and how do we then try to alleviate those fears? Given media stories on situations like the South Carolina mother, along with parenting magazines that equate good parenting skills with having a solid grip on children's activities, parents understandably feel anxious about parenting. This is precisely how the moral panic begins and continues to perpetuate itself, and thus results in what I call the playdate phenomenon.

With the media placing death and disaster at the forefront of their news coverage for the primary reason of selling more newspapers or winning coveted ratings for television, as noted by the sociologist Pierre Bourdieu, the secondary effect is that parents become paranoid about their children's safety. Media consumption on the whole has changed socialization.[13] According to Bourdieu, the conformity and censorship that affect what is shown on television or written about in newspapers are directly correlated with the lack of job security in the field of journalism and news media. This structural corruption of the media is a result of competition for market share (ratings) that simply results in a sensationalized newscast that lacks a critical analysis of reality. In other words, the news as it is presented gives the audience a *sense* of reality instead of a true reality. Parents are consumed with the fear of failing their children and, as the economy continues to fail parents at this time, the middle-class social anxieties that many of these participants expressed make them feel as though they are losing ground.[14] As Manhattan mother Cecile stated, the anxiety has to do with "parents feeling that their children will need to compete in some world market." By taking control, then, of a child's schedule, parents can alleviate some of this angst. Understanding this angst requires us to delve deeper into the differences between children's play in the streets with neighborhood kids, which is potentially dangerous, and playdates, which are more organized and seemingly safe.

Play versus Playdate

The sentiment among most participants is that play is somehow substantively different from playdates. The parents interviewed described the differences quite concretely, illustrating that they are in fact two separate forms of play. Only one male parent, thirty-one years old and living in the Upper East Side, recalled that he heard the term "playdate" as a child. All of the other parents and participants said that they had never heard the term "playdate" until they were much older and actually could not recall when they first began hearing the term being used. For many, it was after having children themselves. Most said that play in their childhood was some form of "free" play, where kids went outdoors on their own to find friends to play with in the neighborhood. Play was defined as children having to make up their own games using whatever was made available to them either in the form of toys or nature (e.g., dirt). When asked to define a playdate, most interviewees said that a playdate was very much a "date" in the way that adults use the term, to mean that you set a time and place to meet with someone specific to socialize. Most playdates started at a specific time of the day that was not nap time and ended either when a child got out of control or when both parents had exhausted their social time with one another (became tired). Most also agreed that a playdate was not something that happened if you met up at a park with someone and decided to let the kids play. A playdate was something that was prearranged either in someone's home or in a setting such as a zoo or a park.

When asked to recollect their time as children and how they played or chose friends, interviewees almost always had the same answers, that a playdate was something created out of fear for children's safety and also the desire to meet people. Crystal recalled that when she played as a young girl, it was "just play. It was never scheduled, when I think about it." Jean was the same. She grew up in Colorado and is the mother of a six-year-old son and pregnant with twins. Now aged thirty-nine and a freelance blogger, Jean reflected on her time as a child, saying, "Our parents would have no idea where we were; . . . it was never arranged, . . . it was never 'And during that time your parents are going to help us to play' whatever, it was very free-form." Comparing simple play with arranged playdates, Jean talked about parents who are "hyper-involved" and "overstructuring" how kids interact. The end result of this, in her opinion, is that children are no longer learning how to deal with hurt feelings or learning what is safe or dangerous. This reaction was shared by most parents who were interviewed.

When parents are involved in determining how play unfolds, children are not able to make decisions, whether bad or good, independently. Play in the neighborhood, where one child knocks on the door of another child to go play, leaves all association up to the child. The children decide on the activities, determine structure, and choose who is going to be part of the play experience. A playdate, however, is managed, scheduled for a particular time, and mediated by adults typically until the children are over the age of eight. In other words, there is little spontaneity and range of experiences. In contrast, in unstructured play, as one interviewee put it, "sometimes you have to play with the bad kid." It is this independence of social interaction that may allow children to develop the skill of figuring out social rules on their own, thus allowing them to function later on in life without the constant mediation of adults. Howard P. Chudacoff, professor of American history, has chronicled the history of children's play according to archival data and has found that over decades dating back to the seventeenth century, "adults increasingly tried to restrict and control children's pleasure by obliging them to follow adult rules, presumably for reasons of rationality and safety. The result was a constriction of autonomous, unstructured, or self-structured play."[15] This lack of autonomy has now been commodified in order to make parents feel "safer" about their children's play.[16]

The playdate is not simple play as Crystal described it; instead it becomes play redefined or a deviation from what used to be seen as "normal" play. "Normal" play for long durations of time involves self-discovery and managing your own time, but somehow playdates seem to become something that is packaged or forced by parents onto the child, making it commodified. Play as a commodity versus play as the commons. This type of packaging or fabrication of a reality can be found in the playdate experience in a variety of places; however, there is one in particular that is truly fascinating in Manhattan, due to the degree to which play is commodified among the upper classes.

Virtual Playdates—The Ultimate Redefinition of Play

In an effort to create "safe" spaces in what is perceived as an unsafe New York City, the elite use other playspaces to capture a more private atmosphere, spaces that utilize technology and an image of green spaces at a high cost. I met up with a mother named Caroline in the summer of 2010 in the Tribeca neighborhood of Manhattan at a coffee shop. I sat at one of the small coffee tables against the wall and watched as kids were brought in by people who appeared to be their mothers or childcare providers. Some children and their caregivers waited in the front seating area and played with some toys that were available to them, while several headed directly to the back of the café.

Caroline introduced herself, we grabbed tea and scones, which were charged to her account at the café, and proceeded with our interview. Caroline is a stay-at-home forty-four-year-old mother of two children, ages six and three, both of whom attended private preschool and had two full-time childcare providers. She is of German, Scottish, and Cherokee descent, is a college graduate, and has an annual household income of $500,000, earned entirely by her husband's employment. After describing to me how she suffers from depression and felt neglected by her mother after her parents' divorce, Caroline proceeded to tell me about how she is raising her own children so that they do not suffer in the way she had as a little girl. Besides the two full-time nannies, and she also had a $1,200 membership at City Babes, an indoor playspace that many upper-middle-class to wealthy parents use on days when they do not want to contend with the weather, but need to get their children out of the house. Caroline said she used this membership primarily in the winter months or when it is too hot outdoors. I asked her about the space we were in, called Moomah. She smiled and said it was one of her favorite places to bring the children, because it is "interactive." "They have a virtual room," Caroline said.

The virtual room is a room for children that has projections of images on the walls and floor that children can interact with. Caroline went on to tell me that Moomah has playdate packages ranging anywhere from forty dollars per child for one hour to sixty dollars per child for two hours. I was bewildered. "What is a packaged playdate?" I wondered. She then led me to a counter where I could find a brochure outlining the various features of Moomah. Before it closed and reopened in 2012 and during the time of this study, you could choose one of three packages, with a minimum of five to ten children depending on the package. Options included the private use of a classroom space; an artist (for example, a guitar player) to guide the playdate experience; and an art project such as making a placemat, frame, or collage. Packages include lunch (either a grilled cheese sandwich, chicken nuggets, or penne pasta), and, for two of the packages, time in the "funky forest" virtual room. Moomah, which was owned by the wife of the comedian and television personality Jon Stewart, promotes these packages as time for the kids to "work off some energy" while parents can be with their "pals" and "spend time enjoying some coffee, lunch and adult conversation." At minimum, Moomah is making $200–400 for a one-hour playdate or up to $600 for a two-hour playdate. Caroline says she goes there for play-dates all the time and even hosted her daughter's fourth birthday party there for over $3,000. The space alone cost her $2,400 for three hours.

I wondered more about the "funky forest" virtual space and Caroline went on to explain how the floor has water virtually projected onto it and then kids can pretend to move the water to the walls, where virtual trees can grow. It is essentially a virtual green space where plants grow almost immediately before the children's eyes, unlike the type of slow growth that would occur in a natural green space. So instead of children going outdoors to play in nature themselves, they are participating in a private playdate, then interacting in a virtual world with people who can afford such an activity. Redefining play and eventual social class reproduction becomes even more obvious with this playdate option. The redefinition of play in this case is the structured and adult-led play in a hyperreal simulation.[17] One might argue then that this hyperreal simulation is the reality of living in a modern urban center where options for redefining play are ample and allow affluent parents to find what may be deemed secure private spaces for their children in order to offset the scarcity of children looking to play on the streets.[18] If parents fear the public commons, they will find new ways to enclose it. This is yet another instance of how parents with financial means can do so. Yet working-class families that were interviewed that did not have the means to secure such private spaces found themselves less concerned with the possible dearth of children in the neighborhood streets (which they never mentioned) and continued to let their children take the lead in finding kids to play with.[19]

What makes Moomah even more unique is that it allows parents to hold an account at the café so that their childcare providers can use the space on their behalf when they are caring for their charges. Caroline said she holds such an account because it just makes life easier for her rather than having to get cash to give her sitters. It is in this context that the café becomes a "safe" space for the upper-middle classes as well as a way to emulate private spaces that exclude those who may not be able to afford such luxuries.

The ultimate question then becomes, how do parents choose "safe" people with whom to hold a playdate? "Safe" in this context really means people/parents who are selected based on potential social and cultural capital. In the following chapters, after describing how playdates are organized, I will argue that parents choose playdate partners based on their social class with the subconscious or conscious intention of ensuring their offspring's future cultural and social capital, thereby reproducing their social class.

2

My Place or Yours?

Playdate Logistics

The house hasn't been vacuumed, there are dishes crowding the sink and piled up beside it as a result of the dinner party I hosted the evening before and was too lazy to clean up, and I'm still screaming from the bottom of the stairs to my kids, who have yet to brush their teeth. Why did I pick this morning to have a playdate when I already have so much chaos at my house? This would be the perfect time to simply call the mother of the child who is coming over to insist that it is nice enough outside for us to meet at a park. Because I know that this mother doesn't approve of kids watching television, I have already made sure to turn off the television in front of which I had parked my kids while I finished cleaning the house. One last-minute prayer to ensure that my son does not end up embarrassing me by coming downstairs in the middle of the playdate in just his underwear, shaking his body like a clown (as he has before). All this chaos only to endure a different type of chaos.

Parents have different rules and different expectations during a playdate. Some parents may be more carefree, letting their children play with toys or each other, but other parents are far more regimented. The one common denominator for all parents interviewed for this project is that parents knew exactly how they liked to approach a playdate, what constituted a playdate, and how playdates ought to be reciprocated.

Most parents agreed that a playdate is an event meant to bring two or more children together for a specific period of time. They also agreed that sometimes it is better to have a first meeting in a public place to feel out the other children's temperament and parents' personalities prior to any in-house playdate, although some parents feel that if a playdate is held in a public place, it really is not a playdate.

Logistics of Public versus Private Spaces

Middle- and upper-middle-class participants tended to agree that holding a first meeting with children in a park was a good idea because there are fewer rules to deal with and fewer issues with sharing toys. Paula, a nursery school director whom I will discuss later in the book, stated that she doesn't believe that every toy should be shared to begin with, so having a playdate in a public place is more conducive to children being able to explore an array of playground equipment or toys that parks may provide.[1] She also suggested that playdates in the house should be monitored and that ground rules should be set early on in the playdate. For example, the host child should put away toys that are special to her/him. According to Paula, "No bedroom doors closed. . . . It's a safety thing; you should check on them. For example, kids will want to play doctor and explore more than others and while the play is fine, you need to set boundaries so that the kids understand what is acceptable and what is not," a boundary my son, who was five at the time, clearly did not know about, nor did I think to set, before he came down naked during a playdate. She continued, "Children are best in the morning because they are well rested. If the child has had a lot of activities, then don't organize a playdate. Check in on the playdate to see if it is going well. Rather than try to fix everything, just change it. Television should be the last resort. If the mother hasn't shown up yet and the kids are getting out of control, then you can turn it on."

For Paula, having a playdate in the park means that you allow your child more freedom—play—whereas if you hold it in a private home, there is a certain level of monitoring and accommodation that needs to be made. In the private sphere of a home, "your children are a reflection of you. There is a range of what people will think is good behavior or bad behavior. The playdate can create tension for parents who want their child to behave one way versus another." In the public sphere of a public park, parents do not need to worry as much about the child's behavior since the kids are off playing with one another, but in a person's home, guest parents are more concerned about whether their child adheres to the hosting parents' rules. Not only that, but leaving someone's home because of bad behavior is more embarrassing than if you simply leave a park. Parents, then, need to be aware that a playdate in a private home may not go the way they had planned, and since the home can be the site of conflict, arrangements need to be made in order to deal with it.

Men and women differed in their choice of a private or public space for a playdate. Men stated that they and the fathers they knew tended to organize more outdoor activities than their wives did. One father named Rick stated that he felt women held more indoor playdates because "they are more social." Rick is stating the obvious gender stereotype that women are more active within the home, meaning they enjoy talking with other parents, while men tend to be more active outdoors (e.g., participating in sports). Even some of the mothers themselves have internalized the stereotype of being more "social" than their husbands and thus holding more playdates in their private homes. This gendered social stereotype has been internalized by both women and men.[2] Previous research shows how women in a patriarchal system are made to feel unwelcome or insecure in outdoor spaces and have been socialized to believe that the private sphere is their domain of control.[3] While some evidence may indicate sex differences that favor women's verbal abilities and stereotypical social roles within and outside the household, others have shown that these differences are merely learned, with no biological foundation.[4] However, with all of this, mothers and fathers in this study continue to view gender in stereotypical ways, thus choosing a playdate space based on tradition—mothers held more playdates in the home and fathers held more outside the home. One mother stated that she believed that "it is so important for girls in particular to feel that there are other adult women that they can trust. This trust is built in the private sphere of the home between young girls and women. When the shit hits the fan, I want her to know that she can call Gail, Tricia, or Jamie, whoever, . . . that they can be trusted with whatever she has to tell them. I'm actively cultivating this. It is not by osmosis, it is something that I'm doing. I want her to know that there are other people that care about her." But it was not just about "other people" in this case, it was about "adult women"; to foster such relationships, she held more playdates in the home, where relationships could deepen and where the space was uncontested.

Teddy and his wife try to juggle their work schedules to not have a childcare provider in Queens. Teddy stays at home during most days while his wife works. When Teddy goes to graduate school to finish his dissertation work on certain days, his wife stays with their son. Teddy feels that playdates have allowed him to get to know other dads who stay home during the day. He said that other mothers do not request a playdate with him or his son, but he is all right with that. None of the fathers in this study initiated home playdates with women unless they and their wives were already friends with them, and even then, most playdates occurred in public spaces such as parks and coffee shops. The men also did not go out of their way to prepare food or any activities for the kids. If food was available on a playdate, then that was fine; otherwise they would go out and pick up something or simply wait until they arrived back at their home to eat. They tended to allow for more "free play" and did not require specific activities to ensure that the quality of play was consistent with that of other parents. In other words, the "performance" of a playdate was less explicit than with the mothers interviewed.[5] Teddy stated that having a playdate requires a serious time commitment and therefore he has them only occasionally with his son, who is just over a year old. Teddy tends to have playdates with one other man, whom he met through his wife's parenting group. She found the group on Meetup. com, a website that allows people with specific interests to get together at various locations. Of the other dad that he has playdates with, Teddy stated, "I'm the same as him: . . . wife works, both into sports, same age." He has met other fathers and couples, but really felt a connection with only this one father and continues to have playdates only with him. Unlike Rick, Teddy believed that indoor playdates were easier because the floor is softer if the kids fall, whereas at the playground, other, bigger kids may run into his son and make him fall on concrete or hard rubber. Teddy's preference for the indoor playdate had to do with how he was constructing the playdate in terms of its social meaning, but also with the practicality of space and potential for his child getting hurt. Teddy remembered growing up with a brother and a yard, a situation where "having a playdate would be silly," but because in New York families do not typically have a yard, they hold playdates instead. He continued, "In the last several decades there has been an increase in safety issues, . . . you know, like stranger danger and kidnappings and child molestations," and so parents prefer to have playdates. Because Teddy's son is still very young, it made sense that he wanted to be around at all the playdates and had concerns about the boy playing at a busy park with older kids. In the same way that mothers enjoyed the playdate experience because of what it provided them in terms of self-identity, Teddy stated that he enjoyed playdates because they allow him to connect with another father who is similar to him and this can help relieve the monotony of the day with a small child. He felt that creating a social interaction with other children earlier is directly connected to the era of Dr. Phil, the self-help talk show host who interviews troubled teens and preteens on his show, as well as the fact that schooling begins earlier for children now with preschool. In Teddy's view, parents hold playdates for two reasons: the perceived danger of public spaces and the early social interaction that may help with social adjustment later on in life.

The playdate, while it is at times a response to the fear projected by the media of children being in danger, is an event that is meant to create more than a shield from fear, it is something parents think they ought to do for their child and, as most admitted, for themselves as well. What appears most attractive about a playdate is the social aspect: the potential acquisition of cultural and social capital for the children involved, and the potential networks for the parents.

Participants all noted that a playdate required reciprocation, although this did not always occur. Fathers seemed less concerned about whether they hosted a playdate, and this could be because they did not typically host a playdate at the house with food and prepared activities. Teddy, Rick, and other fathers stated that they did not concern themselves too much with where playdates occurred. They preferred to meet up outside the home, but when they did host in the home, they typically did not think too much about which home it should be. Again, they were exemplifying men's ability to feel comfortable in public spaces and concerned themselves less with the logistics of what would be considered a stereotype of a "woman's domain," where women nurture their children. Another argument could be made that these fathers hold playdates outdoors more than indoors because they are exerting a presentation of self, a presentation that suggests they are capable of parenting a child, that they are not predatory or untrustworthy, that they are sensitive to their child's social needs. Their public persona may explicitly combat gender stereotypes men face when out with their own children or the children of other parents. Mothers, on the other hand, had very clear requirements when it came to reciprocating a playdate within the home.

Rohan, a Filipino father who works as a lawyer in Manhattan but lives in Brooklyn, was the only parent in my study whose child never has playdates. Rohan's father is the primary caregiver during the day and speaks only to Caribbean childcare providers. When I asked Rohan why he thinks his father speaks only to them and not other parents, he stated that he believed "it is because they are part of the same immigrant story," since his father migrated from the Philippines decades ago. Rohan's two-year-old daughter was getting ready to begin a playgroup in their condominium, where the parents hired a teacher to organize six children during the day for a few hours.[6] He stated that at this point he may begin holding more formal playdates, although he doubted it since the neighborhood kids all live in the same building and see each other all of the time anyway. He said that they don't call it a playdate when they live in the same building, they "just come over" or rather, "play."

Cecile, who lives in Manhattan with her husband and two children, ages thirteen and six, said flat out that a playdate is something that occurs in the house. Even though she works full-time leading food tours in the city (where tourists or other groups go to various restaurants) for forty to fifty hours, she still holds playdates for both kids in the late afternoons and on weekends. Cecile said that reciprocated playdates tended to occur more with stay-at-home mothers than working mothers because their time was more flexible. A stay-at-home mother could pick up Cecile's children after school and have them over to her house while Cecile continued to do her tours. Cecile would reciprocate in the later afternoons or on a weekend to show "good faith." Despite her work hours, Cecile's children were not excluded from playdates because she had cultural capital through her job (access to high-profile restaurants) that other parents sought connections to. She also was particular about the types of mothers she held playdates with, because she understood that mothers who were home during the day could offer her free childcare.

Building Community

This sense of socializing and community building is one of the reasons why playdates in the home are so important, according to parents. Mothers in particular cited how living in New York City itself requires this type of cultivation because it is hard to just land in a welcoming community where people trust one another. The playdate is part of the active work being done by parents to cultivate this community and sense of belonging.

Parents discussed the ways they set up an initial playdate to begin the community-building process. Since most of them have come to know the term "playdate" through other parents or their children's school friends, they often use the term loosely to mean an array of activities, including meeting at a restaurant, going to a museum, or going to someone's home. The majority of participants agreed, however, that a playdate is something you hold at the home of one of the parents. They also acknowledged that their children have come to understand the playdate as something held at a home, not at a park. When asked how they invite someone over for a playdate, many stated that they would do it in person when they drop their child off at school in the morning or pick up the child in the afternoon. Typically the parents will meet either at a school yard or at a public park when they are there with their children. Parents will begin to talk to one another, especially if they notice their children getting along. They come to know that it is the person's child because the parent will talk to the child, or the child will go over to the parent when they need help with something. The parents have a good sense of who belongs to whom, unless they mistake a childcare provider for the parent.[7]

For childcare providers, the same type of interaction happens, but typically with other childcare providers. Also important to note is that kids who take a bus to school or are dropped off by others are already excluded from such interactions. As well, there is limited crossover interaction between parents and childcare providers, as will be discussed.

Parents usually begin with discussions of the age of the children, how cute they are, or how challenging it is to get the child to do something. Once parents begin to commiserate about a topic, the conversation then typically leads into slight indications of what the person does for a living, or whether they are a stay-at-home parent during the day. Depending on that interchange and if the kids seem to enjoy each other's company, the conversation may lead to where the parents live, and after an invitation to one more meeting at the park, it is determined whether a playdate may be a good idea. One parent usually will offer to hold the playdate at their home, especially if they know they have the space for children to run around. Some parents said they determined whether or not they wanted a playdate because they could see at pickup time from daycare or school that the child had a connection with another child. They would then ask the parent in person if they would like a playdate after speaking with them for a while.[8] However, the majority of participants said they used e-mail, telephone, and even Facebook or Evite (an electronic invitation) to set up playdates. Such correspondence would include date, best times so as to not interrupt naps or mealtime, best time of the day for that child's temperament, and location (my place or yours?). The invitation may also indicate that parents should bring their own food due to allergies or special preferences. Some thought that parents usually brought their own snacks for their children unless it was known that snacks would be made available, but most expected snacks to be provided. The act of scheduling these get-togethers at a home through formal invitation qualifies them as playdates.

The fact that most parents contradicted themselves at various points about the definition of a playdate (indoors versus outdoors) suggested that there is social capital and class reproduction at work. By calling all get-togethers "playdates," parents could (1) justify the get-together as something special for the child, although, according to parents, the child understands a playdate to be something that occurs in the home; and (2) use language that is seen as a class marker. The term "playdate" has connotations of middle-class and upper-middle-class privilege (since the parent has the leisure time to facilitate the playdate and the resources to host it), while anyone can simply go to the park. Parents are essentially giving more meaning to the word by expanding its definition to ensure class status—the more playdates, the more social acceptance one must have, otherwise why are parents not calling it "coming over to the house"?

While most playdates occur in the home of one of the parents, there are other meeting places where parents agree they could meet and call it a playdate. Some parents will go to a museum together; others have gone to the American Girl doll store in Manhattan (where the child may walk away with a one-hundred-dollar doll); some go to parks, playgrounds, or grassfields, or go skating; and others meet at cafés, movies, or restaurants. Depending on the time of year or the activities available, playdates can occur anywhere, with varying associated costs. Most playdates occur in the neighborhood where the children attend school and in the home of one family at a time, but there are exceptions.

Both job schedules and transportation issues can be deterrents to holding a playdate, especially if the parents work in a different borough or live outside the neighborhood. Many parents talked about their childhood and growing up in the suburbs or in the Midwest, where everyone drove a car or two. Tracy, a mother of three children in Brooklyn, described the challenges of living in New York as a "city mouse, country mouse battle." Raising small children in New York, Tracy said, requires "a lot more schlepping of stuff. You can't just open the door and allow kids to go out to create their own playspace. It is much more organized and structured and therefore more work" to create a safe space for children to play. She and other parents also talked about the fact that in the suburbs, midwestern towns, or Long Island neighborhoods they grew up in, parents have cars that allow them to connect with others more easily than in New York City proper, where a parent and child must take a subway or bus to a playdate if they don't drive. The upside to living in New York for Tracy is that there is so much more to do. She sees her family from the Midwest as more isolated, whereas in smaller neighborhoods in New York, if you walk and go to the park down the street, you will bump into several kids and parents that you know.

Sharing Labor: The Playdate as Support

Carmela, a mother I interviewed at a local bar in Red Hook, Brooklyn, said that she and a group of women who met during birthing classes got together beginning when their kids were all around one to three weeks old. She stated that she needed to be around other mothers who were going through similar milestones and emotions. When asked how they would initiate a playdate for babies who couldn't even hold their heads up, she said they would e-mail or call each other and agree to meet at one of the women's homes and then rotate from one home to the other over the course of months. Carmela said that each woman would bring either wine or a baked item to the playdate and then lay the babies beside one another while the women talked. It was a chance for them to socialize with somebody who had, or was going through, the same experience of giving birth, breastfeeding, dealing with the sleepless nights, and so on. While Carmela's case seems to be a gathering of a "mommy group," she insisted that they called it a playdate. The use of the term is an inherent class marker since it is something that middle- to upper-middle-class parents say to emphasize that the event is for the children. If this playdate was more about emotional support and counteracting the isolation of new motherhood, then why not simply call it what it is, a "mommy group"?

By conducting interviews with mothers who have children ranging in age from babies to adults, I was able to determine the progression of a playdate. It appeared that playdates eventually turned into something slightly less social for the parent and more practical as far as the daily chores and duties of the parent went. For these women, the playdate starts from early infancy. Then it keeps morphing into something else. As one parent put it, "I want my child to be part of some kind of group at school and some socializing in this very particular way." Usually, by the time their children are five years old, parents prefer to just do drop-off playdates: "Can you pick up my son after school and can they have a playdate and I'll pick him up at such and such time." Then it turns into a network of parents who will do things for each other, who will babysit for free, so that there is no need to have a babysitter. This creates a level of reciprocity, a reciprocity that is typically associated with poor working-class parents who need to depend on others to help with free childcare, because a parent is expected to return the favor of caring for a child while the mother goes off to take care of other responsibilities. Upper-middle-class parents boasted about the time they were able to devote to playdates unlike their working-class counterparts who had to work all types of hours and rely on other family members or paid daycare. However, in reality, these upper-middle-class parents eventually resorted to relying on friends they developed through playdates as free childcare providers for some of the same reasons as working-class parents.

Elizabeth, a Jewish mother who self-identified as "very Caucasian," lives on Long Island and has two kids, aged five and nine.[9] She said that parents she knows now exclusively do drop-off playdates, in which the parents do not need to come back for four to five hours, because the kids are older. This time allows the parents to go shopping, cook, clean the house, or get other work done, similar to what working parents have always done with family and friends. In Brooklyn, some parents are members of cooperatives, which help them get errands done without children.[10] In this arrangement, parents are allotted chits (an amount) of time that they can accumulate if they have taken care of someone's kids for a certain amount of hours per month, and then in turn can use their chits with another family, which returns the favor. It is an exchange of time with no cost. A parent does favors for another under a more organized umbrella, which works effectively as the "village" needed to raise children,[11] and then other playdates happen outside this cooperative babysitting so that the parents can socialize.

It is in the initial years of the child's life that the playdates seemed to be more intense for parents. When asked what the expectations were for playdates, they said that the activity had to be something all parents agreed on, and time was a big consideration for whether a playdate could happen. Most mothers agreed that they would only put their child in a social situation that they could see themselves in. The other interesting point brought up by mothers is that punctuality and the expectation of being entertained by the other parent were paramount in deciding whether a subsequent playdate would occur. Fathers in the study did not seem to care too much about such matters. Granted, the men in this study tended to either not have playdates at all or have kids who were still infants or teenagers/college students. These stipulations were echoed by other participants throughout the study.

Many agreed that parents who worked (especially mothers) or lived outside the neighborhood got the short end of the playdate experience. Parents recognized that not all of their children's friends lived where they went to school, and many families had to move once they were priced out of buying or renting a home in gentrified neighborhoods. Mothers often felt that once they began working more hours outside the home, their playdate frequency decreased. In fact, this tended to be when mothers would opt for a drop-off playdate after school. Both Anna and Carmen agreed that they now seek out only drop-off playdates since their work hours have increased. Carmen called playdates "a blessing" because she doesn't have a babysitter and works, so she will have friends pick up her daughter after school for a playdate until she gets home from teaching yoga. She said that being a single mom requires her to juggle work commitments with childrearing responsibilities. Both Carmen and Anna also feel better about the drop-off playdates, since their children are at an age where they can articulate the events of the day, such as whether something uncomfortable happened. This is interesting since there was so much talk from all parents about the safety of children as the reason for participating in playdates, yet parents feel the need to justify the drop-off playdates to other parents, including me as the researcher, once they begin to work more hours. For example, Carmen said she usually will do a drop-off playdate anywhere from one to three times a week based on her needs because she works, but then she said, "I'm usually present, but I think it is equal, I drop off as much as I am present." However, the drop-off playdates appeared to occur more when she detailed how many days were spent doing drop-off versus other playdates. She appeared to want me to know that she is a present mother, though her circumstances require that she have what she calls "me time." This "me time" also meant free childcare for this single working mother.

Also, this free childcare, perceived by middle- and upper-middle-class parents as something that working-class parents *have* to do, is masked as a playdate, and this again is a class marker to put parents at ease about their childcare needs. Parents often expressed the need to have time to themselves to get things done in their lives, but only the working-class parents were up-front with me about needing a free helping hand, whereas the middle- to upper-middle-class parents always described dropping their children off at someone else's home as a playdate, although they described their needs in the same way as the working-class parents. Many of the Caribbean childcare providers I interviewed for my previous research who were mothers expressed how they had to rely on free childcare from friends or family members in order to survive on their slim wages. Without "free" childcare, which is how they described it, they wouldn't be able to do the work they do for middle- to upper-middle-class families with more disposable income. Even Carmen, who is of working-class economic status, framed her daughter's childcare as an unsupervised drop-off playdate since her social circle (informed by her work contacts) is middle- to upper-middle-class. In the interview she called it free childcare, but when speaking in general terms about what she was doing, she maintained that it was a playdate since they were held with middle- to upper-middle-class families. She was, however, quick to say that the families she held playdates with were different from her: "They pretty much all have their Ph.D.s, they all have more than one child, they have been with their husbands forever, whereas I'm a single mom, never been married; that alone is huge." Somehow the word "playdate" itself became a marker of class differentiation and inequality. Framing the need for free childcare as a playdate was often the way these parents got around their own guilt about what others might think of them.

While Erin's family household income is over $250,000, her mother is helping Erin and her husband put their kids through both private school and college and also with their brownstone mortgage in Park Slope. Erin, a self-identified WASP from the Midwest who currently works as a researcher for a nonprofit organization, discussed playdates with me in her living room while her husband was downstairs. In the earlier days, she said, it was "the mommies that needed to get together. Early on I just wanted to be with other moms to make sense of what was happening to my life, make sure I wasn't the only one losing my mind or losing her sense of her former self." Erin's expectation that there would be a social reciprocation between mothers confirmed what other mothers in this study stated. There was certainly a socialization between parents that

Erin anticipated as she set up her first playdate, when her daughter was just four months old. These initial playdates consisted of sitting the kids on the floor together to have them look at each other or the mothers breastfeeding together. Erin's mother comes to visit her from the Midwest and always remarks how they never had playdates when Erin was a baby. Erin said that her mom at times will criticize her by saying her life is like a gerbil wheel, with people coming in and out for playdates all of the time, and that this lifestyle is not necessary. Erin confesses, "It was more for me, but at least at the time I felt it necessary for my daughter to be with other kids. For her [mother]—not necessary . . . for me—supernecessary." Erin goes on to suggest that playdates now are not about her wanting to get together all of the time with girlfriends, but more about the kids and the activities they want to do together.

Many mothers discussed this need to have time with other women who were new mothers. It became therapy for many and something that got them through the days with a newborn. Some would drink a glass of wine together to take the edge off or simply gossip about new parenting articles they had read, or about neighbors and schools. They found this to be the time where they could commiserate with others in their position while at the same time determine whether they wanted to build long-term friendships with these folks.

One mother stated that "everyone needs a free babysitter," and so parents typically ask one another if they could watch their kids for a few hours while they go run an errand. Anna stated that she always expects a playdate to be reciprocated, especially if it is a drop-off. It is one of the ways that playdates contribute to creating community, according to Anna.

Sherrie agrees that community is built through this socialization. Sherrie lives in a co-op apartment near Prospect Park in Park Slope, Brooklyn, and is raising two daughters, who go to private school. Sherrie and other mothers felt that playdates are phasing out as their children get older. Sherrie believed that with homework increasing each year, the playdates become less and less frequent. She said that the kids in her area are an "ended group," which she admits sounds elitist but is nonetheless the case: they are affluent and in a bubble of sorts, both economically and physically, given the location.[12] When they go out on playdates she may pay for an ice cream cone or a movie ticket for the other kid and does not want the parents to feel obligated to give money to her. She felt that because of their socioeconomic status, the parents did not discuss the money that was spent on a playdate. There was an assumption that the kids would all be taken care of in all regards. According to Sherrie, it is "polite to invite a friend to a restaurant with you." Sherrie's playdates seemed to be centered more around an outing that costs money, but at the same time she stated that money is not necessarily discussed, leading me to assume that if the playdate is reciprocated, she expects the same from the other family. This shows that status and financial security are not a consideration for the playdates in which she and her children participate.

Scheduling the Playdate: Reproducing Class and Status

Playdates have become such a marker of status that businesses are beginning to flourish around them. One mother, discussing how this scheduling has really gotten out of control, described finding out about a business card service for children: "It's so New York. I saw the craziest thing. I was in a coffee shop on Flatbush and there was a classified ad with a picture where a kid gave another kid a business card. It was a business to make playdate cards for kids to exchange with their information on it. . . . It is so Park Slope. It is so brutal. Why is it not just play? The business of play . . . overthinking it, it turns it into something more structured. It's not like Chicago where you could roll outside and have a million kids outside to play with. We live in a different world." The statement that "it is so Park Slope" equates this gentrified neighborhood (which boasts brownstone housing costing upwards of $4 million and dense upscale restaurants and boutiques) with the more extreme fringes of the playdate because of the socioeconomic status of its residents. It also means that there is an exclusivity about Park Slope that would create a demand for business cards that could allow children to pick and choose whom they play with while excluding those who "do not belong."

Of course Chicago is not exclusively a city where kids go outside to play (Chicago parents, too, hold playdates). However, after looking online to see whether business services related to playdates do indeed exist, I came to realize that there are several national companies now offering business cards especially for playdates.[13] Parents can either have the business cards pre-filled with their address and phone number or have cards with blanks to have others fill out if, after meeting another family at the park, parents decide they would like to plan a playdate. What is important about this is the anticipatory socialization of the business card exchange, which prepares children for the corporate or professional world. Christine Williams, author of *Inside Toyland*, studied two toy stores, a higher-end store and a typical box store, to understand the dynamics between shopping habits and work, using an intersectionality analysis of class, gender, and race. She found stark differences between white upper-middle-class and working-class consumers in how they purchased toys and interacted with staff. Using Lareau's analysis of class-based parenting styles, Williams shows how upper-middle-class parents encourage their children to purchase toys in the store in order to confer the class-based advantage of feeling comfortable with monetary exchanges. This, just like teaching children to use business cards to arrange playdates, may be one way that upper-middle-class parents reproduce class simply by giving their child autonomy when it comes to financial exchanges. However, working-class children are often sent to the corner store with money in hand to purchase items for parents as well. Further investigation would be warranted to make any concrete claims of autonomous monetary exchange by children having anything to do with class reproduction. Treating a playdate as a business is perhaps the clearest distinction between play and playdate.[14]

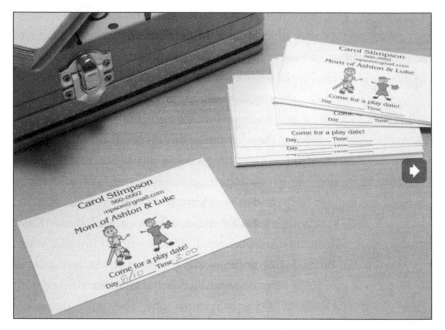

FIGURE 2.1. Family Stickers is one company that offers custom playdate business cards for parents and children to solicit playdates with other families.

Parents said that they are less likely to hold a playdate with a mother who is working during the week simply because there is no time to do so unless the mother finishes work by the time school ends. Most working parents, including those working part-time, said that they hold playdates either immediately after school or on the weekends, like Teddy's wife. Beatrice, a Learning Center director from the Caribbean and mother of a one-year-old, stated that the parents who bring their children for care at her center from 7:30 a.m. to 6:30 p.m. are doctors and typically do not hold playdates. She wasn't sure whether they did so on the weekends, but she said that she would normally hear if someone did have a playdate. While Beatrice says she understands that they need to work long hours, she does not think that it is good for the children. Most parents in this study agreed that they were holding more playdates when the kids were younger (between newborn and age six). By all accounts of participants who had older children, once the children were settled in a school and reached second grade, parents were less likely to go out of their way to meet new parents or hold as many playdates. Likewise, once parents returned to full-time work, playdates were less likely to take place unless the parents held contract positions with more flexible hours. This means that playdates are a useful networking tool for a parent who does not work full-time, but once the networks are in place, the playdates become less frequent. Again, it has less to do with the children and more to do with the parents' convenience.

Transportation was also an issue for parents living in New York. While one mother on Long Island stated that all of her playdates require a car, due to the sprawl of the suburb she lived in, others in dense Manhattan or Brooklyn found that it was much easier to attend playdates within walking distance. Those in Manhattan and Brooklyn suggested that it was too much trouble to have to take the public transit system just to have a playdate, because you would have to tack on an extra half hour just to travel one way. They also talked about how difficult this would be in the winter or on rainy days. What this meant was that the children would in effect have playdates with neighborhood kids, but it also meant exclusion for students who were bused in to school or came from economically different backgrounds and lived farther away from gentrified neighborhoods, or those who moved from the local neighborhood into another. This exclusion, then, would mean that those children not living in the neighborhood of their school could not take advantage of the social networking that was going on with the other kids who did live closer to one another.[15] From the interviews, I gathered that those living outside their school district did not tend to have playdates with their neighborhood's kids. A further burden for some parents is that they would have to make the effort to organize a weekend playdate so that their kids could play with someone living in a different neighborhood. The reason this can be a burden is that many families are together only on the weekends due to work schedules and other activities. Adding a playdate to this typically infringed on the time that a family would have with one another. Participants stated that they absolutely never hold a playdate on the weekend because that is their family time. The complexity of time management and transportation can affect a child's integration into the playdate experience and a parent's networks or access to resources.

The "Bad Playdate"

Once a time, location, and date have been organized and the playdate begins, typically food is offered to both parents and children. Some parents may have prepared crafts for the children to engage in or toys that are selected as age-appropriate, whereas others simply have the toys in an area where kids can choose whatever they want to play with. If the kids get rowdy, some parents will turn on the television; others will leave the playdate. Some host parents may send a visiting child home, and as stated more commonly, the playdate situation will just never be repeated. Erin stated that her daughter "learned a lot of crap from the boy next door. He's just testing everyone and she's picking that up and I remind her that it is not okay." Erin and the next-door neighbor's mother have an understanding that they are to parent the children as they would their own kids, so when the boy next door gets out of hand, Erin tells him, "You're going home now." On another occasion, someone else's son had no control over his own body and would let his arms and legs fling around regardless of what was around him. Erin said, "The mother was there but not parenting. She just thought it was cute. She was just so used to her son being like this. We don't want to have a playdate again. Sure, let's get together, but let's do it in groups and in public like a park." Erin made sure that she did not have the boy over to the house again, and now opts instead for a public space playdate to avoid confrontation and potential damage.

Another mother living in a brownstone in Brooklyn with her two children, who attend public school, had an experience with what she called a "bad playdate." The playdate consisted of more children than the average playdate, which most agreed would have two to three children.

There were three boys and two girls at this playdate, including her own girls. The mother indicated that the boys played rough with the girls and the parents did not discipline the boys for their behavior. One of the daughters of this mother began to play rough in response to the boys. By the end of the playdate, the kids were all crying because they got hurt, toys were broken, and the mother was worried that her glass lamp or television could get broken. This was the end of the playdate, and she vowed to not hold any more playdates with that many children at one time, and especially with that family.

So, although parents may have begun to develop friendships with the parents of other children in the "me date" stage, these friendships could develop tension around a "bad date" that ends in chaos. The sense of parental obligation to host other parents and/or children can often be halted if a playdate goes awry, as in the case of the mother who had too many children on the playdate or when a parent does not reciprocate playdates or does nothing to discipline their own child, a topic taken up later in chapter 4.

Playdates can end for various reasons, but the one most cited is when there is any indication of violence, when the child is being cranky or shows lack of respect for the other person's space, or as Anna, an upper-middle-class Jewish mother, described it, when it is the "witching hours" and the child is tired and becomes unglued at a certain time. When parents relinquish responsibility from parenting, then other parents are not interested in continuing the playdate.

Carmen, a single mother of a four-year-old daughter, gave an interesting account of her playdate experience with a mother and her son. They have had three playdates in total; two of the three did not go well, so they no longer hold playdates together. The first playdate seemed to go fine, but the second one, when both mothers took their children to the movie theater, there were problems. According to Carmen, the son of the other mother was running around and leaning against velvet ropes that are used to separate areas. The mother was present, yet did nothing to effectively reprimand him for his behavior, although the security guard had warned the boy about leaning against the ropes. The son would not listen to his mother as she tried to speak with him calmly, and Carmen's daughter then began acting up. Carmen warned her daughter about her behavior and she stopped; however, the son of the other woman continued being rowdy. She then saw another boy close to him and he began to squeeze this other boy's arm tightly; according to Carmen, "his face changed, . . . it was awkward and the mother just sat there." Later, after the movie, Carmen agreed to take the son to her place for dinner while the mother ran errands. The kids were playing in the other room, when the other mother returned and confided in Carmen that she had previously put marks on her son's face (meaning she had hit her son in the face) and become abusive because she didn't know how to control him. Carmen gave her the number of a professional that she could speak to and ended the playdates with them for a while.

A few months after the last meeting, Carmen thought that the mother had already sought out help since she had said that everything was fine. But on the pickup of the third playdate, knowing how the son can behave, Carmen asked her daughter at home whether anything out of the ordinary had happened. The daughter said that the other woman's son had inappropriately exposed himself to her. Carmen asked her, "What did it look like?" and the daughter replied, "White."[16] Carmen was taken aback and explained to her daughter that it was inappropriate for anyone to show private parts to her. Carmen was also upset that the mother had told her that "everything was fine" and trusted her daughter's story of what took place. This behavior made Carmen believe that the mother hosted playdates for ulterior motives. She said, "Yes, they are helpful, but I just felt like she was doing it not to make her life easier, but so she kind of wouldn't, like, have to deal with her son." The mom told Carmen how her daughter handles her son so well, but Carmen said to herself, "It isn't her job to handle [your son]" since the kids would keep each other occupied and she wouldn't have to deal with her own son's behavior by herself all of the time. Because Carmen did not want her daughter being used for what she perceived as this mother's selfish needs, she stepped away from that relationship and has ended all playdates with that family.

The mothers interviewed in this study often felt, as do mothers in general, that they could not take on all of the responsibility of taking care of a child and, when pushed to their own limitations, would seek out other parents to divert that stress. In this case, Carmen empathized with the other woman as a single mother, and although she understood that the other woman's son was out of control at times, she wanted to help by taking the son for a playdate to allow the woman some "alone" time. This empathy was met with a confession at the conclusion of the playdate that demonstrated to Carmen that she could only help this mother so much. So, instead, she removed her own daughter from the potential dangers of both the boy and the boy's mother entirely.

On the other hand, even when the child no longer wants a playdate with a child who offends them or makes them agitated, some parents say that they continue organizing playdates with the family if the parents are close friends. Parents admittedly "force" playdates on their children for the sake of the adult interaction. Some parents have stated, "We'll just have to get used to the situation" of having the children not get along, since the parents do not want to end their own friendship. Yet other parents will continue getting together without the children when they don't get along. This can also be stressful, since both parents will then either need to find childcare or arrange for a drop-off playdate. Anna, the thirty-nine-year-old upper-middle-class mother living in Brooklyn, said that she had a horrible playdate with someone she worked with in her children's toy company. The other child came to the home and Anna's daughter began acting strangely—"primal," as Anna put it—because she would growl at her. At the time the children were only four and did not seem to connect. They were not engaging with one another, and Anna's daughter began to cry due to the territorial arguments. The following day at the playground, when she saw the little girl, Anna said to her daughter, "Hey, why don't we have a playdate with her?" and her daughter said, "No, we are like a snake and a mouse." Anna asked, "Who is the mouse?" and the daughter answered, "She is, and I want to eat her." For the next few months, Anna's daughter did not want anything to do with the other girl. While the other mother wanted to continue having play-dates, Anna did not, but she said it is difficult since she has a working relationship with the mother and, according to Anna, "It's a relationship that I need to maintain."

Even though Anna's child clearly wanted nothing to do with this other child, Anna did eventually give in and hold another playdate in order to maintain her professional relationship with the mother. It became clear from this case that the playdate had little to do with the child's wants and needs and more to do with the parent and her professional networking, a sentiment shared by many of the upper-middle-class parents in the study. The upper-middle-class parents mostly wanted to continue with playdates even if the children did not care for one another, either because the parents shared a work relationship that they didn't want to risk losing or because the parents really saw the children as a tag-along to a friendship that the parent was building for social and professional purposes. Some parents even stated that that they knew the other family shared similar education levels and philosophies of life and therefore wanted to make sure their children were exposed to them, even if the kids themselves couldn't yet appreciate it. Again, parents held playdates for their own "dating" experience that had little to do with their child's wants and needs.

Most mothers felt the need to reciprocate the playdate so as not to put the onus on just one family. Yet others said that if the other person had a smaller space, they would offer up their larger home to host the playdate. The absence of a reciprocated playdate in the home to many mothers indicated either that the person's house is chaotic and messy, or that something else is going on in the home. The absence of a repeat playdate often meant that the kids or parents did not get along or that the parents were simply too busy "trying out" other parents who may have more of a connection with them.

In all, fathers and mothers understood what a playdate meant, how to go about setting one up, and where it should take place, and they determined the rules as they went along. The social and cultural capital that parents were reproducing through the playdate had already been established, given their knowledge of how to organize and host a play-date to begin with. For the most part, parents wanted their children to feel safe and comfortable and wanted to have some type of meaningful interaction themselves with the other parents. The logistics of a playdate seemed clear to all respondents, even to those not having them, like Rohan. It is through such logistics that parents could determine whom they would continue to build relationships with through playdates, and thus whom their children would build friendships with. The selection begins of who is in and who is out of the friendship group.

3

Who Is In and Who Is Out?

Obtaining Social and Cultural Capital through Inclusion and Exclusion

"Mommy, can you call Lola's mommy and ask her if we can have a play-date?" I want to indulge my daughter's request. But although Lola's mother has invited us to a birthday party that we attended, I wasn't sure how I felt about having them over to our home. Lola's family "appears" to be working-class. Her mother wears tightly fitted black jeans with bright yellow stitching, a tightly fitted T-shirt that puts her cleavage on display, large earrings, and a lot of makeup. Her hair is dyed red, messily tied up in a scrunchie, something I haven't seen many in my circle of friends do since the early 1990s—at least not in public. Her father always appears angry at the world. I thought they lived in the housing projects since I used to see them walking to school from that direction. I had no idea what her parents did for a living, nor did I ever make the effort to find out. All deductions were based on my own stereotypes. How could I indulge such a request after being brought up in a West Indian household where class was constantly discussed as a marker of people's worthiness? I knew as a sociologist that this was despicable behavior on my part, but the reality was that I was socialized to be concerned about introducing my daughter to a class beneath her own. Was it because I felt she'd have enough to deal with as a black girl who may eventually be stereotyped herself, or was it more than that? Maybe I didn't see how this family could further my child's future—a child, admittedly who was only five years old at the time and couldn't care less about her future! I never did end up calling Lola's mother, though I waved to her each morning in the school playground. Soon enough, my daughter stopped talking about Lola altogether when they moved in to different classrooms and entered a new grade.

In this chapter, I show how participants internalize the "People Like Us" concept and act on it through the playdate. I also demonstrate how social and cultural capital are used to create boundaries in the playdate experience as parents construct activities for their children, and how one set of boundaries can create further boundaries, as evidenced in the data.

"People Like Us" (PLU) is a phrase I heard from one of my colleagues one day when we were discussing the topic of this book. The term refers to people who are similarly marked by class or ethnic status based on appearance, employment, or educational and material assets. After interviewing several parents, I came to realize that many were creating boundaries for their children based on their own intention that their children socialize with people of their own class. Class is a complicated distinction in terms of its attributes and boundaries. Some economists may use family household income to determine class status; others may use cultural capital that has been gained over time, such as education, position, or activities of daily life. Others use both. The sociologist Margaret K. Nelson has gone beyond the typical working-, middle-, and upper-class categorizations to develop an even more distinct "professional middle class" group, which she details in her book *Parenting Out of Control*. In Nelson's work, those in the professional middle class have a higher degree of educational attainment (beyond a bachelor's) and have professional occupations, while members of the middle class have bachelor's degrees and what she calls "semiprofessional" occupations. The working-class are further differentiated as sometimes holding an associate's degree and various occupations. As part of the exclusion process that will be discussed, ensuring that playdates consisted of PLU seemed to have more to do with the parents' interests in another family than the child's interest in another child. Most parents initially said that their child made the choice of playdate partner. While this was sometimes the case when the children were between the ages of three and four, it was less so when the children were either infants (and the playdate was more about the parents) or attending school, when it was more about class status exposure.

The PLU phenomenon meant that parents were specifically choosing kids to invite to a playdate based on the parents' outward appearance, including race and ethnicity (for mostly the white families) and class (dress, education, or speech). The sociologist Annette Lareau explores high-status behaviors, attitudes, and preferences that are used for social and cultural exclusion.[1] These class markers include the number and quality of children's activities, parental education levels and employment, and sophistication of vocabulary.[2] For this chapter, I looked at the playdate specifically to unravel how it is a site for exclusion based on class and cultural markers such as education, food, and disciplinary and play styles.

Of those interviewed for this book between 2010 and 2011, twenty-four worked more than thirty-five hours a week in full-time positions; eleven worked part-time up to thirty hours a week or worked freelancing; and only six didn't work outside the home or were wealthy enough to not have to work due to their partner's income. Given that 85 percent of the forty-one interviewees worked anywhere from twenty to fifty hours a week, it was interesting that most were still able to hold playdates throughout the workweek despite their children attending school or childcare and then having organized lessons (unless the playdates were organized by the nannies). Yet, of those who were parents, all but one stated that (1) they never grew up having playdates themselves, and (2) they still found the time to include playdates in their already busy schedule. Some of these middle- to upper-middle-class parents had flexible schedules while working as artists or freelancers, so they worked only a few months of the year. This flexibility allowed them to be home with their kids a little more than those working full-time. It was mostly those parents who discussed being able to network at playdates and who tended to hold more playdates. Parents used playdates, or at least made sure that they continued playdates, with those they felt connected to in terms of their potential or current careers. As one interviewee stated,

"While this is opportunistic, it is also not parenting when it's not in the interest of your child but your own interest that you have a playdate in order to gain something from it." This same person pointed out, "If I were a parent and I knew that someone who had some connections that I could use, well, it doesn't hurt to have a playdate. . . . So it is, I mean it's, as much as I dislike the word 'class,' it is a class advantage in that way."

This form of intentional networking has the effect of redefining play. The playdate is not only a way for parents to find others to socialize with, but a way to achieve personal career gains as well. It may be that the attained class and social capital (the number of networks) gained by the parents are what lead to the networking in the first place and that it is, therefore, a continuous cycle.

Five of the six newer and more affluent parents in Carroll Gardens, Brooklyn, stated that they purposefully did not hold playdates with the longtime Italian working-class to middle-class residents of the neighborhood.[3] For example, Anna, who holds a master's degree and owns an extremely successful children's toy product line (as indicated by her $500,000 annual income), didn't think playdates were necessary for a child's socialization, but set limits on her child's playdate choices. She gave an example: "There's this one little girl and she's very sweet and they're friends at school and that's totally fine, but I've seen her dad, who I don't believe lives with the mom, at the park and he was drunk and totally, like, not paying one bit of attention to the kids and on his cell phone screaming, and I totally broke down. And even [my husband] was like, she [Sally, their daughter] is never having a playdate over there. . . . The mom, we see her yelling into her cell phone, and I'm sure she's yelling at the dad because I know they have some issues, . . . so I'm happy for them to be friends at school, she's a lovely girl and we see them at the park all the time and I'm okay to see them there."

In this case, Anna was more concerned about the safety of her own child if she went to the other girl's home, but I wondered why then wouldn't she invite the girl to her home. Anna said she didn't want to "deal with that" and was happy to simply have the kids play at school.

This was understandable given that Anna was not interested in entertaining parents who would possibly be hostile to each other. Yet it was only the fact that the father displayed his anger and lost control in a public space that deterred Anna, not the child. However, on another occasion Anna admitted that she also never has playdates with the "old-time local parents" of Carroll Gardens, and she indicated that was because of her own stereotypes of who they were as people (rough, loud, and rude). There also seemed to be something safer about having Sally play in a public space, where there are more people, than in a private space, where Anna might feel less secure if a parent was unruly. But this was not really about personal safety, as Anna portrayed it to be; it had more to do with the fact that losing control in a public space is, for her, a marker of the lower class. She had discussed moments in her own home when she yelled at her children, yet did not see this as problematic (she was not drunk on these occasions, as the other parent appeared to be). Other parents suggested similar reasons to Anna's for choosing certain families to hold playdates with.

One mother who lived in the same neighborhood as Anna stated that since her three children are mixed (Indian and white), she often sought out other mixed children and Indian children specifically so that her children would have exposure to diversity and their own culture. She said she was not interested in playdates with those parents who grew up in the neighborhood. Most of the secular Jewish families, such as Anna's, stated that they try to foster relationships through playdates with other Jewish families in order to maintain the religious affiliation, but also hold playdates with other families that do not share their religion, but do share class status. When asked why they seek out other Jewish families, they stated that they grew up with other Jewish kids, who shared in their bar and bat mitzvah celebrations, and they wanted the same for their own children. Other parents from the Greek Orthodox or Catholic faiths said the same about wanting their children to share their childhood experiences with language and rituals. In these cases, as in years past, religious and cultural ritual reproduction determined the choice of friends.

People Like Us parents like Anna also demonstrate how many of the other parents in this study felt about what playdates could do for them. Playdates were a way for parents to connect with parents who were in similar fields or could offer some type of resource for their business. Anna invited other parents over for playdates and had her children befriend certain children in order to have access to the children later on for photo shoots. These photo shoots were considered prestigious since the products (mainly high-end toys) being shot were used as compensation for appearing in the photos and normally retailed at a high price point. During one of the initial playdates, Anna also found out that one mother's husband was a set designer, and she began using him for the actual photo shoots. However, when the man was no longer being hired for the photo shoots because of Anna's new creative direction, that relationship was severed for several months, causing tension between the children, who later stopped having playdates. Anna and this mother wanted to confer advantages on their children and ultimately both families through association, yet when a business decision came between the families, leaving the husband without a promise of future income, the friendship ended. This "business" arrangement ended the children's friendship, a friendship that had been building through several playdates.

Parents are able to create a bounded space for the playdate to ensure that social distinctions are reinforced. In New York, parents actively shape the playdate in order to preserve class distinctions by sorting people by culture, language, religion, education, and general lifestyle choices.

What do we mean by social and cultural capital? As discussed in Annette Lareau's work, which builds from the sociologist Pierre Bourdieu's initial definitions given earlier in this book, those who garner social and cultural gains through their networks or interactions with certain groups of people will most likely have positive outcomes, especially in education. These gains tend to come from concerted middle-class cultivation. "Concerted cultivation" is the practice of middle-class families that use "organized leisure activities and extensive reasoning" to parent their children. These are the parents who engage in playdates.[4] For example, Lareau posits that those with high socioeconomic status tend to be more familiar with education systems and therefore tend to have a more positive experience with schooling, something that I discuss later in this chapter.[5] In addition, Lareau and Horvat state that "students with more valuable social and cultural capital fare better in school than do their otherwise comparable peers with less valuable social and cultural capital," a value determined by the parents themselves.[6] This capital, then, continues the cycle of allowing "middle-class parents . . . [to] plan the system," thus gaining personal advantages for their offspring. If social and cultural capital are explained in this way and economic status and its subsequent exclusionary features become the marker for who is allowed access to these forms of capital, then we can say the playdate can become a site for class reproduction due to the potential future capital gains of a certain group of parents and children and the necessary exclusion of another group of parents and children.

Lareau and Horvat's arguments resonated with my interviewees in the educational field: two New York City elementary public school teachers, a college professor of children's studies, and two private childcare center directors. Teachers agree that positive experiences of middle-class groups (and conversely, the more negative experience among working-class groups) translate into an educational experience that has specific outcomes. These outcomes include the reproduction of social class, something that teachers would like to reverse to a degree, yet find themselves enabling. By taking on the perspective of educators, we can see how they too shape the play experiences and opportunities of children.

Children have been invited out to playdates at second homes outside New York City where parents have pools and large yards. This too is how children and parents may benefit from knowing the "right" type of families with exhaustive resources. Social class is reproduced through such encounters, which determine who belongs and who does not. However, these invitations tend to cease if the parents end their relationship. Again, it is not necessarily about the children's relationships, but the parents' interests and what these interests can confer on their children at various moments.

Thus, social and cultural capital gained through the playdate experience can be shaped through parental involvement. In the earlier years, parents determine whom their children will play with and when. As the children age, they may have more say about whom they choose for their playdates. However, many of the parents in this study claim that by the time their children are able to make these choices themselves, their circle of friends is usually already established. Parents maintain that they are able to find time for playdates despite the hectic schedule of activities they already maintain for their children and believe that it is necessary for their children's social connectedness and future development. Even the teachers interviewed for this book claim that the benefits of play dates outweigh the potential exclusion that they may cause. It appears, then, that parents and teachers alike enjoy the role of matchmaker, see concrete benefits to having playdates, and have little issue with adding another activity (the playdate) to an already extensive list of planned activities so long as they can personally benefit from the activity and have their children gain something from it. What is interesting is how other forms of play become devalued in the face of redefined play.

One father (who came across as having a higher level of understanding about child development based on his work at a charter school) gave an honest assessment of the contradictions in his and his wife's approaches to playdates on behalf of their four-year-old son. Franco, a self-identified ethnically mixed Italian American (a term he did not clarify) whose wife also works at the charter school where he works, talked about his neighborhood in Brooklyn, where diversity is advertised by area realtors. He said that his child is able to "see the call to prayer by Muslims in his neighborhood, and Orthodox Jews walking to temple." Despite the diversity of his children's public school, he has not been able to have playdates with these particular populations because he is culturally and religiously different. One day his wife asked a South Asian Muslim woman whether she would come over to have their children play together since they appeared to get along so well in class, but the woman said no—"especially if I'm there," Franco said, meaning because he is male. He believed it was "something cultural," because when he has attempted to shake hands with a Muslim mother at school, a natural and automatic greeting for him, she didn't extend her hand in return. He suggested that "immigrants may not have the language for playdate," and he thinks that "white people or American white liberals" probably started the term in the first place. He remembered being called a Park Slopian by the Russians who lived in his previous building, even though he had never lived in the pricey brownstones of Park Slope.[7] He added that the Russians, who maintained sensitivities about the gentrification going on in Brooklyn, had this idea of him as a yuppie liberal white person, even though he grew up working-class.

Those parents with whom Franco has had playdates share, as he put it, "this economic level," which for him was around $200,000 annually, and "this sort of level of education," meaning a master's degree or professional degree. He went on, "As diverse as my group of friends are that we have playdates with, they are all very highly educated people. Those that don't have that same level of education, I don't have playdates with them. . . . I go drinking with them or dancing with them [the less educated parents]. My kids don't play with theirs." Franco echoed what stratification research has shown for years: "an offspring's subsequent attainment is highly correlated with the education of the offspring's parents."[8] Franco, then, consistently and consciously sought out playdates with highly educated parents who would reinforce his children's social capital attainment in both school and in the home, social capital that has been accumulated over time by such families. Unlike himself, Franco said, his wife did not currently hold playdates with people below her class level because she has "a very high standard for the quality . . .

not in a judgmental way, but in the qualities that people possess, and those are the people she associates with and more likely have a playdate with." Even their nanny will only hold playdates that "are beneficial to the children." He admitted that his friends from his past had convictions or did drugs and then related that he had a good friend with whom he got together every now and then with the child. His friend swore offensively at his own daughter, but Franco said that he makes an exception with this friend because they have history together. Franco also stated that his brother, who is from a lower economic class, came over with his child as well, but it is his brother, and they too have history. Again, Franco illustrated that if the parent wants to have an interaction badly enough, that trumps the child's feelings or the type of environment that a parent is willing to put their child in. He determined who was in and who was out. His friend and brother were in, despite their class, because these were People Like Us in other ways. As he put it, after describing how playdates are performances where people are judging one another, much in the same vein as Goffman's frontstage performance, "If a child is smacking your kid, you're not going to have another playdate with them, unless you are really close to the parent and then you'd try to work it out." Franco is performing for certain groups, allowing a projection of who he is in one setting to comfort the group he is currently engaged in, even though he may behave differently in another group. In other words, what is acceptable on one playdate would not be acceptable on another, depending on whom he is performing for. In Goffman's frontstage performance, a person projects an image of themselves that is accepted by the audience as convincing. A performance is given (in this case, a parent performing for another on a playdate) and the audience (the corresponding parent) determines whether the performance was believable. This forms the basis of the interaction throughout the playdate.[9]

Anna admits the same about "working things out" with families. As discussed in a previous chapter, Anna and a colleague arranged a playdate that turned sour. Despite the child's feelings about how the first playdate went, for the sake of the parent's potential future relationship with another parent, a playdate could still occur, thus forcing a child to create a relationship that would not otherwise naturally occur. This is reminiscent of the earlier discussion of the sociologist Markella Rutherford's work, whereby mediation stunts the autonomy of children to make their own decisions about whom to have playdates with. Again, while Rutherford suggests that the mediation primarily occurs by surveillance in the public sphere, I argue and illustrate how this mediation is also prompted to occur in the private sphere of the home.

While this all appears to be intentional on the parents' part, Joseph, the children's studies instructor, has suggested that perhaps it is not all intentional. He stated that parents are "following patterns and they're following what they read in magazines and they . . . don't want to be the parent who's not doing it." He went on, "You risk a number of things. You risk being that parent who's weird. I recently spoke with a mother who was telling me that she felt so ostracized because she was taking her child to see *Kung Fu Panda 2* and everybody else is like, 'Well, that's a violent film. *Kung Fu Panda 2*, that's violent, why would you take your child?' And so this group of parents was policing her for that sort of thing and it was commonly understood that, well, watching violence has some sort of negative outcome, therefore, we collectively agree that that's not something we should really do and it's really strange that you're doing it." In this case, the woman was being told that "she's out" of the homogeneous group that believed *Kung Fu Panda* is violent. She also felt that by not complying to the norms set by other parents, she would be seen as not like the others, "not like us," and that this may somehow impact her child's and her ability to continue socializing with that group of parents.

Patterns of inclusion in and exclusion from the playdate are something that parents learn from the reinforcement or disassociation by other parents. As Franco said of the parents he mostly held playdates with, "their level of education, parenting philosophies are the same, parents who have postgraduate education and work in professions that are 'good.' Meaning teachers, social workers, people in politics, but are about uplifting people. . . . They are like us." Maria, the mother of two in Manhattan, agreed, saying that the parents she approaches for playdates have a "certain education level" similar to her postgraduate degree. Parents pick and choose from their class and are drawn to that group, retaining their association with people like them while distancing themselves from those who do not conform to the same class values unless they are a blood relative, have some type of history with the person, or have something to gain professionally.

TABLE 3.1. Calendar for Author's Kids, Spring 2011

MONDAY	TUESDAY	WEDNESDAY	THURSDAY	FRIDAY	SATURDAY	SUNDAY
SCHOOL 8:45 a.m.- 2:50 p.m.	SCHOOL 8:45 a.m.- 2:50 p.m.	SCHOOL 8:45 a.m.- 2:50 p.m.	SCHOOL 8:45 a.m.- 2:50 p.m.	SCHOOL 8:45 a.m.- 2:50 p.m.	DANCE LESSON (daughter) Ballet and HipHop 10 a.m.- 1 p.m.	SOCCER Practice/Game (son) (1 hour varied)
	KUMON LESSONS (daughter) 3:15-4 p.m.		WEEKLY ALLERGY SHOT (daughter) 3-4 p.m.	KUMON LESSONS (daughter) 3:15 p.m.- 4 p.m.	SOCCER Practice/Game (son) (1 hour varied)	
PIANO (son) 3:10- 3:50 p.m.	TAE KWONDO (son) 4-4:50 p.m.	PIANO (daughter) 3:10- 3:50 p.m.		TAE KWONDO (son) 4-4:50 p.m.		
PICK UP FROM SITTER 5 p.m.	PICK UP FROM SITTER 5 p.m.	PICK UP FROM SITTER 5 p.m.	PICK UP FROM SITTER 5 p.m.	PRIVATE TUTOR (daughter) 4:15- 5:15 p.m.		

Benefits to Overscheduled Kids?

I thought that my own children's calendar for the spring 2011 semester would shed light on what overscheduling might look like. Looking at it in this form actually frightened me, given that I had not included the additional two or more playdates per week. Not only are my kids involved in something other than school and homework, as they should be, based on my class value judgments, but these extracurricular activities take place on every single day of the week. More than that, it is mostly my childcare provider who chaperones them to these various lessons, except for Fridays and the weekends, although this has changed in recent years. How is it possible that I became one of "those" parents? Am I a product of my social circle? Am I worried that my children won't have enough interests to keep them busy? Worried that my daughter's math skills won't get her into a good New York school? Or am I desperately attempting to fit in? Perhaps it is simply the fact that from ages five to nine I was enrolled in piano, dance, recorder, guitar, and school sports teams. Out of all of these, dance was the only thing that stuck with me for life and actually turned into a career after a long battle to do well in school. But maybe the exposure alone allowed me to sift through my interests, create relationships, have the confidence to pursue a Ph.D. like my father, interact with a variety of people, and establish my family as middle-class. All this . . . and for me, no playdate. Those who have been socialized to network already know how to cultivate relationships, whether it be on a playground or at a playdate, so the playdate could be (1) a place where parents gain a career advantage, and (2) a place where parents who already have established social capital can simply act upon it further because of their class status and thereby exclude others from their social circle. Another benefit of playdates, besides the potential networking between parents, is the social capital gained by the children themselves. While I cannot make claims for the children of the parents interviewed, some examples may illustrate this social capital gain.

Parents who engaged in the playdate experience tended to have some expendable resources, had their children signed up for various activities, and worked with a rigid weekly schedule.[10] So the schedule might look like the following: school during the day or daycare, music lessons, dance lessons, soccer practice or some infant/toddler playgroup, religious lessons, and then summer camp from July to September. When participants were asked whether a tightly packed schedule for children was a benefit or somehow disadvantaged children, the answer really depended on what the measure of success was. While researchers might agree that the overscheduling effects on family function are unclear, others suggest that participation in such activities has more to do with parents than the enjoyment of the child.[11] For example, as one interviewee put it, "If you think about success as making six figures and having a car and 2.5 children and a home and so on, then it would be good for their success, but when you consider mental health, personal adjustment, and everything else, then it gets a little more murky for me." A 2008 Child Trends brief states that indeed the overscheduling myth is just that, a myth. There are few overscheduled children to begin with, and for those involved in several activities, there are more positive effects than negative on a child's outcome.[12] In his time as a marketing researcher, Joseph, the children's studies teacher, stated that he saw the struggles of younger researchers in his company who felt entitled to immediate success, but couldn't achieve it as quickly as they had hoped. He stated that most young applicants are "fresh out of college, . . . like, they look like they should be the CEO. They have wonderful résumés; they've spent time here and spent time there. They had internships here, they had internships there. But when they come in, they don't have any creative skills and everything is just tactical, putting this here, putting that there, and no critical thinking." All this makes the effort of training these young researchers more stressful and less rewarding. Joseph's analysis does not mean that piano lessons are worthless, but what he alludes to is that parents and their children who come out of college are concerned more about the appearance of skill than the child's development of critical thinking. The increase in disposable income for upper-middle-class and upper-class families has allowed these children to develop in material and social ways (travel to multiple countries, have computers, and take a variety of lessons, gaining cultural capital through social networks), yet has deprived some of them of the need to think critically on their own and creatively solve a problem without adult intervention.

On the other hand, being socialized in an adult's world can have certain benefits. Joseph articulates how the son of his former CEO was able to integrate himself with a senior class of people. He "walked in like he owned the place, he sat down, they shook hands, they chatted, they were having this wonderful conversation, very easygoing; he felt at home being with this CEO." The meeting went extremely well because the assistant was comfortable with someone at that level, probably because his mother is a CEO and she is well connected. Joseph added, "I'm sure they all have dinner and lunch and everything else and that he's been there the whole time and when his life is run by adults and being scheduled here and going there and having a nanny and everything else, he's just so comfortable with adults because he never had a world of children, and so it worked out beautifully." While Joseph states that the young budding executive "never had a world of children," he later acknowledged that they had been children, but they were the offspring of high-level professionals and therefore did not necessarily act like children. They were children emulating adult concerns and learning how to network based on that interaction.

In this case, the CEO's son had been socialized by being around high-level executives and their offspring at an early age, so his meeting with another CEO did not faze him in the way that it had fazed Joseph. The social benefits, then, came with the network into which he had been socialized. This is age-old class advantage, where the son had the opportunity to socialize in such a way because of his exposure to high-powered people. It is this exposure on which parents in this book seem to want to get a head start. Parents calculated the advantages of the networks to which they would expose their children and made sure to put their children in lessons that reflected that network's class, for example, fencing classes, piano lessons, and academic tutoring. By scheduling their children in precise ways, parents believed they were ensuring their children's own future network. This network is furthered directly by educators.

Teaching to Playdate

When I spoke with the two founders of a website service that connects parents of special-needs children to arrange playdates with one another for a monthly fee, it became clear to me that social and cultural capital were of the utmost importance. Without generalizing to the larger population of teachers, focusing on these two teachers and later in the chapter, bringing in the voices of other childcare center directors, I was able to better grasp how educators influence the playdate experience, what benefits they ascribe to the playdate, and how contradictory their opinions can be. Melanie and Linda teach grades K–3 in New York's diverse public school system. For them, trying to form groups and enable children to work together as co-teachers and to promote social learning (learning from each other) can be difficult because they are constantly trying to "get everyone on the same page in terms of what is appropriate behavior and what in general was socially acceptable." This was especially challenging when they team taught a class in a lower socioeconomic neighborhood. According to Melanie, parents were nonexistent and "students came in malnourished or not dressed appropriately for the day's events, and this impacted their social development." It was this state of affairs that gave the two teachers the idea for their website, which would connect children with special needs with other children outside the school (with or without special needs) so that they would be more integrated with people outside their social class. They determined that students needed exposure to different experiences.

What seemed to be missing from the teachers' understanding of social class (non)intermingling is that parents created enclosures of the commons, in this case playdates, in order to maintain and reproduce class stratification to a certain extent. These playdates would exclude those not in one's class and could also exclude those with special needs. We see this in previous chapters when parents discuss maintaining ties with certain types of families through the playdate experience in order to afford their children certain class privilege.

In the classroom, these teachers merged children from different social classes in order to create community among the students, a community that the teachers stated was lacking beyond the school's doors.
They also stated that the students were getting "no warmth, no love" at
home. I explained to them that perhaps different groups show warmth
and love in various ways, and they admitted that there were definitely
multiple meanings of warmth and love. In asking Melanie and Linda
about playdates in particular, I was curious to know whether they
found that some children might benefit from the playdate experience
in the way that Joseph had explained the benefits of a network. I also
wanted to know why these teachers believed that we have gone from
play (something that participants claim all children used to do and that
is now associated with working-class children) to playdate (something
that participants say more middle- to upper-middle-class children do
that is circumscribed by their parents). The two teachers define a playdate as any setting that has "two children or more and is facilitated by
an adult to promote social skills or academic skills," which differs from
this book's definition.[13] Melanie, who was twenty-seven at the time and
lived on Long Island, explained how the involvement of parents today is
more important than it was in previous generations. In this precarious
economy, there are different pressures in terms of career preparedness.
There are higher expectations for children to do well in school, and most
students will need to go on to college since there is more competition in
the workplace. According to Melanie, it was this competition that created the playdate.

Depending on which area of New York you live in, you would see
children playing differently. In East Harlem, the kids tend to just go
out on the street to play, with less adult supervision. The two teachers
suggest that playdates are happening in more affluent neighborhoods,
where after-school programs are organized, and that "parents are push-
ing their kids onto other parents so they can get a break," as I found in
chapter 2.[14] What they are finding is that the students who are higher
academic achievers are having playdates together, but more surprisingly,

the students who are lower academic achievers are "playing" together. In other words, the kids who are in the projects together play together at home either with or without an adult present and are typically not having the play "facilitated," while the students who live in pricier high-rises or brownstones are playing together in a more formal playdate, where a parent or educator is moderating and "facilitating" the play (organizing activities with the intention of facilitating learning). As I have said earlier, the parents are simply reproducing their class advantages and ensuring networking opportunities through the playdate experience, but so are educators to an extent. Parents may be mediating play, but not necessarily facilitating it. However, in these two groups of students, subgroups are being created based on academic achievement. Melanie did go on playdates when she was younger and said she played what she describes as "some type of educational game," and wasn't allowed to watch television if a friend was around unless it was a movie. Monopoly and Boggle are seen by her as educational because they involve the counting of money, spelling, and a rudimentary understanding of property acquisition, sale, and rent. Her mother would do arts and crafts with her and her friends on an organized playdate. However, Linda, who is Asian, did not have playdates but rather played outside where there were no adults present. She says her ability to use expressive language is very different from that of her business partner who, she believes, is more articulate. Linda strongly believes that playdates would have helped with her ability to communicate. She stated, "I think the playdate is the most natural setting a parent can create for the child, to support and practice social and communication skills." This contradicts Joseph's statement that simple play with neighborhood kids is actually the most natural form of play, and this itself will lend to social and communication skills along with real-life experiences that one cannot gain while on a playdate if it is moderated or, as Melanie puts it, "facilitated."

Beyond this, no one had yet mentioned the difference in material conditions of the different families, which clearly would set varying trajectories for children. If the material conditions do not allow for "street play," then children may find entertainment through video games or watching television, with little interaction with other children or adults since it is not necessary. On the other hand, if the material conditions of a household provide board games or other forms of communication and general social capital building requiring adult mediation, then the children in those homes may interact differently in life.[15]

The fact remains that the more privileged children are playing with the more privileged, while the working-class are playing with the working-class. While housing affects whom one could play with, it also means that a class of children is not having much contact outside school with other classes of children, and thus the divide is perpetuated. This divide is something that the two teachers find within the school structure as well.

As New York City schools change curriculum, Melanie finds that the new educational strategies are somewhat stifling children's ability to progress educationally. New York City public schools have implemented recent changes to the curriculum in order to address the failings of the United States compared to other countries, especially in math and sciences. This new core curriculum focuses on abstract thinking and learning strategies, as opposed to the older model of rote learning. Unfortunately, it is still too early to determine the concrete outcomes of the new curriculum changes in New York City, though we do know that the new Common Core state test scores were lower in 2013 than in previous years.[16] She claimed that the new curriculum for early grades is "all about play, where children can freely interact with toys," but that if she takes a step back as an instructor, she has to wonder where the direct instruction, which "definitely worked," has gone. However, if one actually looks at the curriculum in New York City schools, one can see that there is more of an emphasis on reading and writing than play, unlike what Melanie suggests. The New York City core curriculum maintains a strong focus on reading level, writing ability, simple computation, and comprehension in earlier grades. The standards have become more rigorous over the years, and do not emphasize play.[17] She stated that children who suffer from the lack of expressive language will be successful only if they are put into social situations, but, ironically, they have to interact within the boundaries set by the facilitators. Because they feel so strongly about this, Melanie and Linda have created stations within the classroom that are centered around play, which contradicts their earlier claim that direct instruction is what "works." However, they feel that even though kids are learning how to communicate and socialize in school, this effort also needs to be carried out in the home, since that is the setting where children lead their daily lives.

During a playdate, according to Melanie and Linda, children learn to work together and ask for help, but according to them, the children they teach do not see this modeled at home, so parents can have their children come to free after-school programs. While this contradicts their belief that the behavior should occur in the home to reinforce what is learned in a school setting, they feel that the after-school program at school acts as a playdate and therefore may be used by families as a resource to help children achieve academically and to learn "appropriate play." Yet what they are forgetting is that the playdate is not entirely being re-created in the school, since parents are not part of it and are not connecting with other parents. A playdate in someone's home and under some other type of parental organization is where the social and cultural capital is reinforced, not necessarily by the public school and its teachers, although as Lareau points out, schools that have a large middle-class staff (and, I would argue, PTA constituency) also promote social and cultural capital among the student body.[18]

When probed about the benefits of an actual playdate from a teacher's perspective, both Melanie and Linda said they noticed the differences in writing skills between children who have playdates and those who do not. Important to note here is that this may merely be a correlation and not a causation—one does not necessarily cause the other to occur, since they did not conduct research with measureable outcomes. As well, they are referring to playdates occurring in a private home, not in an after-school program. Socially, in the classroom, those who have had playdates will talk to one another more and discuss things that happened on the playdate, while the ones who are not engaging in playdates are feeling left out and therefore speak less in class. Melanie said that in first grade, the children keep a journal where they can write stories about events and their lives; these journals reveal a difference in the level of writing. The teachers suggested that "the children who have playdates with other children tended to write more and have a level of detail about events and emotions that go beyond those who do not engage in play-dates." These same children also tended to write more pages, thereby giving them more practice with writing in general.

There was no mention throughout this conversation that social class may have anything to do with the fact that some children are able to detail their experiences in written or oral form more than others or that they have been socialized to do so. As Lareau points out in her stud-ies, working-class children are often told not to speak up about their personal lives at home and not to engage with adults about children's activities.[19] She states that "the sense of an obligation to cultivate their children that is so apparent among middle-class parents is uncommon among their poor and working-class counterparts. Likewise, the sense of being entitled to adult attention that is so prevalent among middle-class children is absent in their poor and working-class peers."[20]

The two teachers continued to explain how some children wrote up two pages while giving detail about their lives outside school. They both found that children gained social and academic skills through playdates because they (1) are practicing their oral language; (2) are executing writ-ten language with detail; (3) can relate to the events in the books they are reading once they get into older grades; (4) can infer more based on experiences and emotions learned through the playdate. However, none of these points have been systematically documented by them or their institution. They even suggest that playdates could help students on the SATs, which their lower socioeconomic students tend not to do well on. "There are questions regarding farms," they said, "and if a student has never been to a farm they will not have the experience to relate to and answer correctly." This did not make sense as they explained it, since playdates are not usually held on farms in New York City, so I did not follow how a playdate could help with such a question. In an effort to better understand the farm reference, I suggested that some children may just not have the financial means to go to a farm, since it would require transportation and sometimes an entry fee. The teachers then stepped back from the playdate argument and said that there is free Internet now at the school and parents need to make use of resources like the library for books and Internet. Again, how a "farm playdate" related to better performance on the SAT was unclear. I was left unsatisfied, knowing that parents living in the conditions that these teachers spoke of might be working night shifts or working multiple jobs and thus not have the energy or time to go to a library to help their child. They immediately said, "You have to give children experiences to promote learning." They believe that despite your economic situation you can go on a scavenger hunt, go for a walk, or go to free events, but none of these necessarily have to do with a playdate. Melanie said that she did not understand parents who stated that they could not afford experiences because she saw the parents or kids with "brand-new high top sneakers" and "parents on five cell phones," basically stating that the way the parents are choosing to spend their income is irresponsible.[21] She also admitted that much more work needs to be done in terms of going into the projects and educating the parents about child development as well as the need for more translators to connect parents with teachers. Again, this was merely a glimpse into how teachers may perceive the population they teach and how parents manage parenting along with the seemingly important impact of private playdates.

Melanie's and Linda's firsthand experience with the benefits that children in their classroom derive from playdates is what catapulted into existence their website, which they are hoping will help foster parental involvement. As directed by their lawyer, they will charge a monthly fee of twenty dollars in order to attract people who are serious about holding playdates for the "right reasons," since the company is not liable for anything that may go wrong (although legally it may be impossible to be free from liability). There is also a stipulation that it is the parent or legal guardian who must facilitate the playdate and not nannies. By including these rules and fees, Melanie and Linda have yet again used the concept of a playdate to reproduce social class.

I found this interesting because I am left believing that the parents who will choose this option will be parents who can afford the monthly fee, afford the time to go on the Internet to search for an appropriate playdate, and afford the time to actually go and be interested in the playdate. There is also a trust factor involved. Trusting a website to connect parents and children could be viewed by some with skepticism. This website will not be for those who appear to be the most at risk in the neighborhoods where Melanie and Linda teach. Those children will perhaps only have the option of participating in after-school activities, which do not, according to other teachers and parents, really constitute a playdate.

Reproducing the Playdate at Daycare

Educators have established the playdate as a "reality," but to what extent is it forced upon parents—and ultimately children—by educators? As I entered the nursery school in Brooklyn on July 16, 2010, I smiled. I passed by the Caribbean front desk workers, who were chatting about the day's schedule, to wait for the school director. The walls were adorned with ocean life–themed art created by the children, and variously sized and colored octopuses appeared to be staggered in a way that led children to various classrooms. In this immaculate space, there were friendly behavior messages hanging throughout the front waiting area, such as "Please be quiet" and "Be nice to your friends." Paula, a third-generation Irish Brooklynite, entered the waiting area to greet me and then led me to her small office just behind the front desk area. She was fifty-five and dressed like a primary school teacher, with a long skirt, a buttoned-up blouse tucked in, and "sensible," low-heeled shoes.

As director of this private childcare center in a gentrified Brooklyn neighborhood, Paula, who is married and cares for her aging mother, discussed what it was like raising her nineteen- and twenty-three-year-old children compared to her memories as a child, and the differences she sees in the way today's children are being raised. Her annual household income is over $250,000 and she holds a master's degree.

"A big part of your leadership role is to keep your child safe, because you have the life experience to know what is safe and what's not," according to Paula. Paula believes safety is why we've gone from play to playdate, yet contradicts this sentiment throughout our conversation. She said that Brooklyn has changed over the years so that it is less cohesive than it once was, even a decade ago. She said, "To just send your kid loose in the street you have to feel like somebody will look after them." She suggested that part of the change had to do with racial integration and people's unwillingness to accept it. The loss of racial cohesion, she says, is also a loss of innocence due to the violence being portrayed in the media. According to Paula, it is this loss of innocence due to violent representations of New York in the media that has changed the way people play, but also people's education level and sophistication have somehow made the city safer now. Even though Paula claims that there is less cohesion, she simultaneously stated that she feels it is more connected today with the middle- and upper-middle-class families who have come into the gentrified neighborhood. These families she spoke of are predominantly white middle- to upper-middle-class families. Despite this lack of cohesion that Paula discussed, she saw playdates as a way for parents to engage their children in play, but more importantly as a vehicle that allows parents to "bounce things off, someone to commiserate, share the happy things too" with regard to parenting strategies. She claimed that playdates are a result of parents being needier than they once were because they are professionals whose families do not live in New York City.

Because Paula believes that parents are needier, she encourages playdates if she notices a child trying to negotiate their social life or the environment. She actively selects children for a playdate experience in the same way that Melanie and Linda do, and says to parents, "Here's three people who might be good for a playdate." This active engagement in constructing the playdate stems from personal experience. She remembered her son being socially awkward and the teacher suggesting playdates, so she re-creates the same experience for the students she oversees in preschool. When asked whether she sees playdates as successful, Paula said she determines the success when she sees an element of the playdate repeat itself in the classroom. Students will say, "Hey remember when you saw my cat . . . ," which then creates dialogue between the students who shared an intimate experience. Paula suggests that building this dyad creates a more positive learning environment for children who are still negotiating their social circles in the same way that Melanie and Linda see children writing about their experiences on a playdate. However, what is interesting is that she is constructing the socialization without the children's input or that of the parents. Instead, she is imposing her opinions about who is socially compatible and who can benefit from whom. While this all happens under the guise of "trying to develop kids' social relationships," it also may force two children together who do not have any interest in each other. Further, there is no evidence that this dyadic experience would not occur in the same way with simple "play." Further, she could also be selecting based on PLU status.

Some mother interviewees argued that their children were set up with other kids with learning needs or felt that the teachers forced their kids together or that the mother in a playdate was left to deal with children who had issues of temperament. Those playdates resulted in a stressed-out parent and child and a sense that the teacher did not know anything about their child's wants or needs. In the same way that Paula describes parents who project their own issues on the child without paying attention to the child's needs, she, too, does something similar when she creates a playdate situation where the parents have limited input. Parents feel obligated to follow through on the playdate since it is suggested by an authority figure, in this case a teacher, and when things go badly, there is guilt on the part of the parent for not having "made it work."

Paula's experience in constructing playdates herself has been that there have not been any negative consequences that have been brought back into the school, especially when there is "extensive networking going on" between parents. It is this networking that mediates some of the negative feelings expressed by parents because there are many opportunities to connect with those who are like-minded. Though Paula helps to organize playdates with some of the kids at her school, she also believes that children are doing enough socializing at school and should have some "down time" after school.

Beatrice, another private learning center director for children in Manhattan, states that although she does not push for playdates among her families, playdates do happen and she sees how happy the children are to have seen their friends at their private home instead of the school setting. She also states that parents appreciate the time together because it gives them an opportunity to talk about what is happening at school and gives kids an "opportunity to see that there is a whole other life aside from what they see in the school." Yet Beatrice, who looks after kids between the ages of eighteen months and twenty-four months, found that once they had frequent playdates together, the kids exhibited frustration because they had spent too much time with their friends outside school and in school. They got "sick of each other" and then would act out in class. Unlike Melanie, Linda, and Paula, Beatrice said that the older kids at the center did not really demonstrate any connectedness in school from the playdate experience and that instead they tended to gravitate more toward kids they did not see that frequently.

So while some teachers and directors see playdates as a positive networking tool that enables social ties in the classroom, others did not necessarily see the direct benefit in the school situation and in fact observed the opposite. However, one thing that all of the education professionals acknowledged in one way or another is that networking also maintains social class positions, since those parents having playdates tend to have similar professional jobs. While children in the daycare center do have playdates with children of different socioeconomic backgrounds, Paula states that those playdates are more rare and typically are held in public settings, not in the parents' home, thereby contributing to the reproduction of social class in intimate spaces and relegating differing social class interactions to public settings where there is less at stake in terms of getting to know another family. In Beatrice's center the same is true, because its location in Manhattan and the high cost to attend attract a certain class of parents, so those playdates occur between the children of upper-middle-class parents who share similar professional positions.

Paula, Melanie, and Linda seem to embody a sentiment among some teachers that there is an unwritten obligation to foster the organization of playdate experiences for children outside the school day in the name of socialization. While some of their comments appear to deviate from any structural conversation regarding housing, race, class, or socioeconomic privilege, they are indeed actively attempting to create social and cultural capital gains for certain children by either placing children together in a playdate situation or attempting to re-create the playdate in the classroom. However, Beatrice does not believe that playdates, whether created by teachers or parents, actually enhance the child's educational experience in any significant way. Creating an interaction that is not naturally occurring is one way of combating the reproduction of social class, but as the children involved are still young and under direct supervision of their parents outside school, often those relationships seem to give way to parental preferences and ultimately to PLU parents.

Class versus Race versus Culture

Culture, not just class, also determines who is invited to the playdate. People from different socioeconomic backgrounds tend to rationalize play in different ways. Those in the higher economic bracket can rationalize sending their children on sixty-dollar playdates at a virtual playspace, as Caroline does, while those in lower economic brackets might use vouchers in order to pay for childcare, not even considering playdates as something that they would want to participate in because it is not part of their vocabulary, figuratively speaking. Lorena stated clearly in her interview that "playdates are a white people thing" and that "playdates take the fun out of letting [children] play. . . . It's a status thing." While Lorena, Franco, and several others said that the playdate was something that white people or white liberals made up, what they are really targeting is the class difference. Interviewees tended to frame "middle-class" as code for white. "Being white" meant a certain level of education, household income, and privilege. Of the families I interviewed, those who earned less than $100,000 annually tended to do drop-offs with friends and family so they could go to work or run errands, but did not necessarily call it a playdate, while those in the higher income bracket did call the drop-off a playdate even if it were for similar reasons. According to census data on adjusted median household income, the majority in the higher income bracket in New York City (and the rest of the nation) is white; black median family income for the second generation is $41,900, while for white families it is $78,800, so it is not too far-fetched to imagine that Lorena would make the comment she did.[22] Others, however, couched their statement about "whiteness" in terms of class, making the distinction between play and playdate and who is in or who is out more about class differences than racial ones.

The stereotypes of playdates being a "white" thing do not just come out of thin air. One thing I noticed throughout the interviews with the twenty-eight white parents (including Jewish participants) is that, when asked who they were having playdates with and how diverse they thought these playdates were, most parents paused and thought for a few seconds, only to recall the one black person that they ever had a playdate with, which was often usually a onetime event. In addition, no one ever mentioned Asian Americans as part of the diversity of their playdates, although I knew that many of them had playdates with Asian Americans, so Asian American families tended to be subsumed into the "white" category or at least the "nondiverse" category. The sociologist

Eduardo Bonilla-Silva states that a spectrum of whiteness has been "conferred upon and actively pursued by Hispanics and Asians as some of these groups have been dubbed 'honorary whites.'"[23] He also states that "whites feel less comfortable living around or marrying blacks as opposed to Hispanics or Asians."[24] Latinas/os were never mentioned either. It could also be that since parents stated so clearly that playdates are a "white people" concoction, perhaps this was a way for parents to reify their white privilege or lack thereof.

Tracy, the mother of three, of whom one is South Asian and two are white, held playdates with "mostly white folks or mixed folks that are very light-skinned. The last few years have now become more mixed as the kids get older. Similar class, similar viewpoint on how you speak to children and goals for kids. . . . I think having kids of different colors in your family, it forces the conversation of race. When my son was really little he would talk about the color of his skin and talk about how he felt about it. My other friends who are white and not in biracial relationships and whose kids are white would say, 'Oh, my kids are just oblivious to race and they don't notice it at all,' and I would say that's because he's white, it's not that he doesn't know his race. It's just a given. . . . It's not that they are oblivious, it is that they are part of that dominant culture. I think the same goes for the parents, they tend to not think about it." So there are definitely racial elements to the playdate and to how people speak of race at a playdate that potentially stem from class, but perhaps also from racial privilege and comfort.

Questions of similarities in material conditions of those having playdates also arose. Those interviewed who consistently held playdates tended to purchase more expensive (wooden) toys for their children, aimed to eat healthier choices such as organic alternatives instead of heavily processed foods, and lived in neighborhoods that were inhabited by "PLU" residents. On the surface it appeared, then, that there was a correlation between the playdate and fancier or more expensive toys and healthier food, but really this was a correlation between the class advantages that allow for the language of playdates and the purchase of expensive items such as toys and organic foods.

David, dad to a twenty-month-old, said that he held playdates mostly with other Jewish upper-middle-class parents who lived on the Upper East Side of Manhattan. He claimed that comfort was the reason, because as children these new parents had similar upbringings and now share similar lifestyles. Diversity for David is important, but he is not concerned right now because of his son's age. He feels that as his son reaches school age, he should learn "there are other people out there besides the ones that are in the city that are the same class or race as you." John stated the same: playdates are organized based on whether or not he liked the parents and had something in common with them. This commonality came in the form of racial background, shared religious affiliation, and economic standing for the majority of parents. Again, the playdate initially is something for the parents and their own socialization and what the parent wants for the child's future life chances. If a child becomes socialized among people like their parents in some "systematic, predictable, and regulated" way, then they too would likely become part of that community that shares class, status, and culture.[25]

If one looks at the opposite end of the spectrum, what Lareau calls "accomplishment of natural growth" for the working class, the parents tend to follow the pattern of just go out, play, make your own games, come back at 5:00 p.m.[26] In this case, the children have much more control over play, can go find children to play with on their own, all while not bothering the adults or expecting them to initiate play activities. I found this with working-class parents in Harlem and Brooklyn, who described their children as having more autonomy to go find friends in the neighborhood to play with and find things to play with that "don't bother" the parents. In this way, there is a distinct class difference: working-class parents do not engage the playdate model of a prearranged time of play. Also, the natural growth method would potentially involve a more diverse array of children, depending on the child's geographic location. While race and class may remain stable in certain cities or areas, children may become exposed to various types of behavior from people during this "free" play. However, and as Lareau has pointed out in her research, the benefits of natural growth do not necessarily translate into an advantage once children are in the public sphere. American society rewards flexibility of skill, ability to think critically, and an attitude that exudes confidence, traits that are found in the concerted cultivation of middle- to upper-middle-class families. Being reserved among adults and subordinated to authority figures, which natural growth can contribute to, is not rewarded.

Another criterion in selection of playdate partners is language. Parents who spoke French at home preferred to hold playdates with children whose parents also spoke French, though in this case, most were in classes together at the same French dual-language school. Still, most of those classes are half Francophone and half Anglophone, so parents were being selective out of the already select group of potential playdate participants. It is unclear whether this selectivity would play out differently for Spanish-speaking families or families that primarily speak another language, since it did not come up in the interviews for this particular book.

Pressures to Conform

Mandy, who is mother to a half-European and half-Pakistani nine-month-old baby, described some of the pressures to be a good parent while on a playdate in her Union Square neighborhood. Mandy went on at least two playdates per week with her baby and organized her baby's playdates through Chat, Chew and Chocolate e-mails, Mommy and Me yoga classes, Bowery Babes, and other open play sessions. Chat, Chew and Chocolate is a social networking site that is meant to connect mothers for playdates, learning about recipes, or events. Bowery Babes is a New York nonprofit organization that brings mothers together for support from pregnancy onward. Judging from their advertising and the language used, I would say that these websites target mothers of middle- to upper-middle-class status. Some of the events require a fee, which again targets parents with disposable income for such leisure get-togethers. The pressures she has encountered have to do with the environmentally conscious parents among moms in her "same economic group." She stated, "Earthy parents don't like toys to be plastic." This preference for nonplastic toys was shared by Emily, who works as a casting director in Brooklyn. Emily stated that she doesn't like plastic toys because of the chemicals she claims they emit. There seemed to be a preference among those earning over $100,000 for wooden toys in their own households, but most would never say anything directly to a parent if they had plastic toys while on a playdate. The pressure comes from claims in the popular media that indicate that plastic is bad for children, while wooden toys such as those made by the company Melissa & Doug are a healthier choice. Perhaps the wooden toys suggest to parents a more authentic material culture of childhood, paralleling what the museum studies scholar Sharon Brookshaw discovered in her museum analysis of childhood (mentioned in the introduction). Brookshaw showed that the homemade toys of children in prior eras were most representative of childhood material culture, yet were rarely on display in museum settings because they were perhaps either too fragile or not considered seriously as having meaning.[27] Perhaps, too, purchasing wooden toys makes parents feel that their children are playing with something that is more "genuine" and handmade than a plastic toy that is mass-produced. For example, a quick search online will show that a plastic easel for children at Toys R Us costs around $55, whereas a wooden easel from Melissa & Doug costs around $80. If one were to buy the same wooden easel from a boutique children's store in New York, the cost rises to around $89–$99.

Other pressures come in the form of playdate activities. According to Battery Park mom Cara, who is of Italian and Spanish descent and married to an Egyptian man, her economically similar playdate friends (her annual household income is over $250,000) are mostly older professional, "organized Type A parents that have their children in expensive formal activities, and pricey private high schools." While she stated that she has racially mixed relationships with other parents, she immediately stated that "there is definitely a white- and blue-collar divide that fosters different worldviews." Cara feels the pressure to keep up with her friends and dole out the money for acceptance among this group of parents, since the underlying message is for parents to do whatever they can to ensure the future of their child. The mothers she is friendly with are mostly lawyers and she says they tell her, "You have to have a nanny." Her having a nanny is the antithesis to what Cara called "dirty daycare" because it costs more. Cara is performing and thus confirming her class status by hiring a nanny at a higher rate than the "dirty daycare." There is a perceived advantage of the personalized attention that her child will receive that lends itself to the class status of having a highly paid nanny. Cara is suggesting that she will pay to ensure that her child is surrounded by PLU at all times due to the peer pressure.

Laura, who is African American and lives in East Harlem, making over $120,000 annually, said that she too holds playdates with people who share similar values and typically holds playdates with stay-at-home mothers who have cars. Given that Laura herself works full-time, it was interesting that she held playdates mostly with stay-at-home mothers whom she stated she wanted "to be entertained by." She was entertained by the standard of living of those stay-at-home mothers, their experiences during the day since their work was in the private sphere, and the fact that she could hear all of the gossip from the parks during the weekdays. Laura said she does not really know people in Harlem and therefore held playdates with people living outside her area of residence, because she saw it as a "class-based" opportunity for her child to play with children outside Harlem.

Parents recounted how children's playdates could become a venue for competition for resources or perceived social and cultural benefit. One father recalled a children's music teacher who held a recital for wealthy "white" kids who regularly have playdates with one another; the teacher did not want to hold a reception afterward because he couldn't "stand these people." He said that he enjoyed the parents individually but was not interested in seeing them interact after the recital, because they all were too competitive when they saw each other's children play their instruments. He claimed that parents started to discuss whose child is better or make statements such as, "My child was playing that three weeks ago," even though the parents see one another at playdates. What made this story more intriguing was how parents who are close enough and similar enough to hold playdates with one another would have some sort of value of their own bound up in their six-year-olds. These first graders were made a symbol of class status by parents for their musical prowess and also victim to the competitive "my kid is smarter than your kid" narrative that parents impose. More important to note is that classical music itself is considered high culture and associated with upper-class status. In order for their children to play an instrument well, most parents need the financial means to purchase often expensive instruments and pay for their maintenance. Parents pay for lessons that cost hundreds of dollars and supplement group lessons with private lessons that could run up to a hundred dollars an hour, depending on the activity. Being able to play an instrument well has always been associated with the middle to upper-middle classes, as have fencing, tennis, and equestrian sports in many cultures, including Western Europe and America. Parents were more likely to engage in playdates with children of similar class status and who hold similar "high culture" values, thus reproducing a class value that lent itself to such competitiveness in the recital. Again, this pressure to make sure a six-year-old performs as well as the others somehow affected the parents' sense of value. It was an event meant to be a nice time, enjoying music and gaining an artistic experience, not necessarily a competition.[28] This concerted cultivation of children as musical prodigies, as argued by Lareau, encourages competition in a structured environment that parents translate into some form of preparation for the working world, as it gives them a leg up in their social circles, ultimately leading to some form of entitlement. In Lareau's work, working-class parents are less interested in this form of cultivation and instead insist that their children experience a natural growth in their more cooperative interactions with neighborhood children or family members. Leisure activities for middle- to upper-middle-class children become preparation for adulthood, while leisure activities for the working class are simply meant to be leisure activities.

Nannies, Playdates, and the PLU Phenomenon

Nannies and other caregivers are also involved in playdates. Working on behalf of the upper and upper-middle class, nannies must find ways to entertain the children they are caring for throughout the workweek. Most do this by creating communities among themselves and sometimes using their employers' homes to host one or more childcare providers and their charges.[29] My fieldwork from 2004 to 2007 with Caribbean childcare providers explored some of these encounters. On those playdates, the nannies would cook food and have the children play with each other, or at least sit next to each other if they were too young to do more than what Mildred Parten calls "parallel play"[30] (play next to each other without actually interacting), while the nannies socialized. These playdates were much like the playdates described earlier. It is interesting to see that nannies, too, are socialized into having playdates with many of the same features that employers have, including a set time, food (although many times Caribbean and not organic), and mediated behavior. My previous work showed that nannies arranged these playdates in an effort to build their own communities and break some of the monotony of their workday, so the research assumption then becomes that parents are doing the same (breaking the monotony). However, nannies typically hold playdates with other nannies, and parents who employ nannies hold their playdates with other parents. As Mandy put it, "Mommies and nannies don't mix." When asked, the nannies I studied said they never had playdates back in their countries and it was not a term they knew prior to working in New York. So the question becomes, how do these caregivers come to know the term and what it means? Do they enjoy having playdates arranged for them or do they prefer to set up their own with other caregivers they know from the parks? Also, how are they contributing to this redefinition of play?

Through the interviews conducted for this book, I learned that employers on occasion would organize playdates for their childcare providers and then the providers were responsible for following up on the appointment. This was usually how the nannies came to know the term "playdate." The term was used by employers to indicate to the nanny that a time and meeting place had been arranged on their behalf. This did not sit well with most providers. They often complained that their employers had set up playdates with either other providers whom they didn't know or with the parents of a child, which really made them feel uncomfortable because they "weren't like them." Some childcare providers held very strong religious views that made them feel uncomfortable around other providers. For example, some providers had dietary restrictions or did not wear clothing that revealed skin on the legs or arms, and if the other provider didn't share those values, it made for an uncomfortable social exchange. Playdates with other parents made providers feel uncomfortable because of the racial and class hierarchy between white parents, who had the luxury of staying home with their children (parents were exclusively white in these cases), and the providers, who were all women of color who had to work as nannies outside the home. Some parents, like Caroline, did say that she sometimes held playdates with providers whom she met at parks, but that they are not typically repeat playdates, perhaps because of this disconnect.

Rick, a Taiwanese father of a fourteen-month-old who lived in Turtle Bay on the Upper East Side of Manhattan, stated that "parents don't have playdates with nannies. . . . Nannies are for convenience . . . but parenting is the full spectrum." So while Rick feels that it is up to the parents to guide the intimate social interactions of the child, he also described nannies and parents as two separate social groups. After speaking to parents about nannies and parents working as different entities, I realized that some parents believed that nannies are not supposed to interact on the level of a playdate, where children are potentially creating meaningful social ties for future social and cultural capital. Some parents felt that nannies should only care for the child and not socialize with other parents because they are being hired to do a job and did not necessarily want other parents to know their business. If a nanny were to divulge personal information to other parents, there would be a conflict of interest. This was not overtly expressed by parents in this book, but it had been mentioned as a concern when parents and providers intermingle. While not all parents felt this way, several articulated this idea.

Crystal, who lives in Tribeca with her daughter and husband, admitted that she and her husband are wealthy enough that she does not need to work full-time while she earns her graduate degree. She claimed that breaking up her time with daily playdates gave her day more structure. Her daughter had a childcare provider for three days a week, and Crystal said that the "nanny would spend time with nannies in the park, . . . always with those she knew." While there are playrooms in many of the Tribeca buildings, Crystal said that the nannies didn't want to be in those spaces and preferred being away from the employer's home. As previous research suggests, the employer's home is a private space where hierarchies exist between worker and employer; therefore nannies prefer to be in public spaces where they have more control over whom they meet.[31] John, who at thirty-five lives in the West Village of Manhattan and earns $400,000 annually, suggested the same when speaking about his eighteen-month-old daughter and the idea of organizing playdates on behalf of his nanny. John stated that "nannies set up playdates so they can go to houses together." Again, and as I found in my research with Caribbean nannies, childcare providers preferred to set up their own playdates. Crystal also noted that the providers preferred to be away from the employer's residence, perhaps for the same reasons that Rick mentions, namely, that the social groups are different.

A nanny can become a "victim" of the playdate when an employer forces a playdate on her by sending her out with other people's children.

George, a realtor with two now grown children (ages sixteen and nineteen), said that he used to send his St. Lucian babysitter to the park with his children and "had her take other children" with her. He seemed to think she did not mind since she never fussed about it, but in fact, as I learned when speaking with childcare providers for my first book, providers did not like it when this type of responsibility was thrust upon them without appropriate compensation. Providers felt that they were being exploited when they were asked to take on uncompensated responsibilities for other people's children on behalf of their employer. They did not feel empowered to say no to additional work because of their subordinated position. Caregivers do not consider it appropriate for employers to make caregivers take care of additional children or organize playdates with people. Most childcare providers told me that they preferred to make their own connections, either because they held strong religious views that were similar to other providers, were not as outwardly social or were cautious about letting others into their lives, or more simply, did not want to be treated as a child who needed to be prompted or organized to socialize with others. Providers sometimes enjoyed the break, but most did not like feeling pressured by parents to interact, let alone take care of another person's child on a playdate that was arranged for them.

Not all participants had access to private nannies for their childcare services. At least two parents held ACD vouchers, now called Administration for Children's Services or ACS, given out by New York City to help pay for childcare services through an agency (and paid directly to the childcare provider). In fact one parent, Lorena, a Dominican and Puerto Rican native New Yorker, said that "childcare and finding a way to pay for it" were one of the downfalls of living in East Harlem. Although Lorena's household income is now over $75,000 a year, she relied on ACD vouchers to pay for the childcare of her three children as she completed her bachelor's degree. Now forty-one, Lorena no longer needs to use the vouchers, since her children are old enough to stay on their own at home. Neither parent who used ACD vouchers organized playdates for the women caring for their children, since they viewed their use of those childcare providers as strictly a service, whereas other parents who did use private childcare perhaps felt comfortable doing so because they saw their providers as an extension of themselves.

While parents organize a playdate instead of simply letting their children go out and play in order to combat some of the fears that they have for the safety of their children, nannies are being asked by these same parents to continue the playdate experience during their workday. Because of the nannies' subordinated position, they often feel that they have to do as they are told by their employers, thus adopting the playdate language and, at times, the perversion aspect (i.e., a completely structured, hyperreal situation) of the playdate that happens in places like Moomah. Although many nannies enjoyed spending time outside the home, being told that they must have a playdate that has been organized on their behalf was not seen as respectful and at times disrupted the community building of the nanny herself.[32] In this sense, nannies also employed the PLU rhetoric. Nannies would prefer to hold playdates with people like themselves, who worked as nannies and shared their ethnic background, and they wanted to organize those playdates themselves using their own social networks. Employers were also interested in making sure their children engaged with people like them by forcing the issue of the playdate instead of allowing those networks to develop on their own through the nanny. Ultimately, the children being cared for by the nannies I interviewed and observed were of the same race, economic background, and neighborhood, so the PLU requirement for the children was met despite the organizer.

From the parents who used ACD vouchers to aid in providing childcare, to the nannies who did not grow up holding playdates with their children, to those encountering virtual places such as the ones in Moomah, it became apparent that there are class differences in how people conceive of playdates and their organization. More than this, parents demonstrated how children's interactions are manipulated or mediated through the playdate experience by the parents' careful choice of playdate friends. Objects such as toys define class status, and thus choices for playdates become class-centered and materialistic. Playdates are encouraged as a means of gaining cultural and social capital for parents and their children and a way to foster urban homogeneity. Teachers and childcare center directors will encourage parents to set up playdates that they deem necessary and perhaps functional for a child. While no research proves that playdates have direct benefits on long-term life chances, there is a distinct belief that this is true.

4

Playdate Etiquette

Food, Expectations, Discipline

I tell my husband that the parents are coming for our son's weekend playdate with another five-year-old, so I have to cook something. His only concern is making sure that we have enough wine and beer.

I think to myself, "What is quick and easy?" Ah yes, my famous stewed
chicken with a salad and the chickpeas and red bean dish. I lay out Mid-
night Moon cheese, some whole-wheat crackers, and a bowl of strawberries that I picked up from the grocery store where most gentrifiers shop
in Red Hook, Brooklyn. I am so proud of myself after standing over the
gas stove for forty-five minutes. Soon, the doorbell rings and the playdate
begins. After our initial greetings and our guests' quick once-over of the
first floor of our house, the first thing I find out is that the husband is a
vegetarian. "Great! All that work and he can't even eat the food," I think to
myself. "Well, at least there are beans and salad." Three of us eat the main
dish, while the husband has to eat cheese and crackers with beans and
salad. Playdates are becoming complicated at this point, and I find myself
having to accommodate the particularities of parents, something I don't
remember my mother ever doing for children, let alone their parents. Three
playdates in one week, and I've fed a vegan, a vegetarian, a pescatarian, and
a friend who eats only gluten-free. At least the kids eat whatever I put out.

Other books have noted that food not only nourishes the body, but
also fosters an understanding of social life through the rituals of
offering and eating.[1] As I had found in my previous research about
Caribbean childcare providers, these rituals create specific meanings
for groups of people.[2] As the sociologist Marjorie Devault argues in

her book *Feeding the Family*, family meals reproduce traditional family norms as well as norms of domination in the household hierarchy, whereby women are consistently placed in a subordinated position. That is, women are responsible for the domestic sphere, cooking and cleaning. Devault argues that the social ritual of feeding in essence creates the family as a social institution.[3] The family becomes an institution through feeding as it is organized to embody specific belief systems and values. Care is demonstrated through the social act of feeding and preparation. In the same way, the sociologist Elaine Bell Kaplan discusses how feeding middle schoolers in the private sphere communicates solidarity with their family, while being fed at school demonstrates care on behalf of the school.[4] According to Goffman, such social rituals become essential to our everyday interaction and help foster our social self.[5] These social selves affect how we perceive our roles in our communities and how others perceive our roles, and can determine our inclusion in or exclusion from certain social groups. I argue that because playdates promote social class membership, the playdate also becomes a site for offering food. While there are practical reasons for offering food to small children on a playdate (and for infants the reason is a more concrete physical necessity), there also are more social reasons for offering food, such as demonstrating culinary competency, proficiency in nutritional education, and ultimately class membership, reasons that apply to the adults who often accompany the children on a playdate.

Upper-middle-class parents interviewed for this book told me that they offer certain types of food, such as organic or non-sugary foods, to their playdate guests that they would not necessarily eat themselves on a regular basis, but that they do this in order to fit in with what is expected of them based on the class status of their guests. These same parents have gone to playdates where chips or soda were offered and knew that this would not be a home to which they would send their child unattended, since chips and soda in their minds were closely aligned with irresponsible parenting by the working class. At the same time, they would not walk away from the playdate if that were the food option, because it would be impolite.

The sociologist Erving Goffman's frontstage and backstage theoretical framework becomes important as we begin to understand how parents navigate food in the context of the playdate. In the frontstage, actors (in this case, parents) are performing an ideal parenting style that projects a middle- to upper-middle-class status, which may include offering higher-end or healthier food options at a playdate, when in fact the backstage parenting they do without an audience (playdate guests) does not include the regular consumption of such items. Performing this frontstage role, Goffman would argue, is when we develop our social self because it is this frontstage that is judged by others. Parents begin to believe their performance and therefore exhibit class savvy. Offering healthier food options on a playdate gives upper-middle-class parents a sense that they are doing right by their children and their guests, and, in certain social circles, offers them a higher-status social position.

The social anxieties about playdates reproduce themselves in the ritual of food offering. Carmela, a thirty-nine-year-old middle-class mother who works full-time outside the home, stated that she always presents healthier choices on playdates. She said there is "pressure to be a good parent. First because you are insecure and you never know if you're making the right decisions, and two, that another parent holds you accountable. Two people together raises the bar. You have to present yourself, . . . who am I today? You want to be a good person so you want the playdate to reflect that you are a good person and show your best self. For me it's, 'I want to show this person my best self.'" She admits that this is stressful, but mostly in a good way, because she sees it as a chance to put her best self forward. For Carmela, the frontstage self offers healthier food in order to present herself in a good light to the parents of those she is holding playdates with, yet her backstage choices (or what she does at home when there is no company) may not be as healthy.[6]

Anna from Brooklyn agreed that there is pressure to conform on a playdate, especially when the parents are with the kids. Anna stated,

"I definitely put out healthier choices than if it were just the kids. . . . I would probably do fruit, but I might do like, um, tortilla chips instead of Cheetos, and if the kids were just here I would just give them Cheetos because they like them. I mean they're orange and so fake. I probably wouldn't bring it out if a parent were coming over." Again, Anna presented a frontstage self that is seemingly healthier by offering tortilla chips while her backstage self might offer Cheetos. Marzenna, a thirty-three-year-old Brooklyn mother of two children, ages one and five, felt pressure when one particular friend, who had changed her entire diet, came over. The popularity of restrictive diets, such as gluten-free, organic only, pescatarian, or vegan, among the white professional class is one that fosters anxiety and pressure among parents. The reason is that these options are often costly, which is a marker of class membership, as well as exclusionary. When a parent is offered meat or an option that is outside the dietary restrictions, the host is then left feeling either insensitive or "out of the know." This can cause a parent to feel anxious about being judged. Marzenna said, "Everything she cooks is organic and gluten-free, it's just the works. I don't even know if she eats sugar or anything, so if she were coming over, I would definitely have anxiety." Luckily, Marzenna had been invited over to her friend's house first, and when she saw that the friend made pizza for the kids, she was less worried about having them over to the house.

For parents in this study, fast foods were seen as the ultimate class marker (fast food equated to working-class), even though most parents, especially those in the upper-middle class, admitted to me that they sometimes give their children fast food, but they were very cautious to not reveal this during a playdate with certain children. Working-class parents did not seem to dwell on the frontstage presentation; they simply brought out food that was inexpensive, would fill the children's stomachs, and made the children happy. The concerted cultivation practiced by the middle- and upper-middle-class parents, which included offering particular types of food deemed "healthy" on a playdate, meant that these parents were socializing their children to expect a certain quality of food when at people's homes, when in reality, those children may be fed fast food or "junk" food when not on a playdate and in the private sphere of the family. Upper-middle-class participants often cited "junk food" as a nuisance due to the preservatives and hormones that they contain. Organic options were viewed as acceptable because they are thought to be more wholesome and without additives. For working-class parents, the natural growth parenting style meant that children could eat what would keep them quiet, happy, and satiated without any effort to pretend that they eat only healthy options. In general, middle- and upper-middle-class parents felt that if people had specific food needs, then they should bring their own snacks to a playdate, and while some said that parents did, many did not because of the expectation that food would be provided by the host parent.

Elizabeth, a Jewish mother on Long Island who works full-time outside the home, laughed as she told a story about not wanting to become friends with a family even though her daughter liked the child, because she used to see the family's kids eating McDonald's or Burger King every day. She said, "I just thought that this is not somebody who sees the world the way I do." In Elizabeth's world, parents should be more conscious of the food they give kids. She stated that she does not like to worry that another parent might bring a "fifty-count of Munch-kins [mini donuts] into the house" when Elizabeth is bringing out bananas and strawberries. Elizabeth did go out of her way to get to know the family and is now good friends with the mother. She said they joke about what she thought of the fast food since they have a comfortable enough relationship now, but the other family does not eat McDonald's around Elizabeth. Elizabeth says of the mother, "She will on occasion let me know if she's gone to Burger King with the kids, but she knows she is not supposed to be taking my kids to Burger King or McDonald's." Now that she has established the rules for her own children, the other mother performs her social role around Elizabeth and only includes healthier choices; however, this performance ends once Elizabeth is no longer present. This ongoing joke about foodways is something that they simply agree to disagree on.[7]

From this back-and-forth between Elizabeth and her friend, it is clear that a food standard has been established based on class and the frontstage performance it projects. It is important to understand how participants defined the food boundaries of class in these cases. Most participants agreed that McDonald's was not a healthy choice, yet going to Starbucks for a large coffee topped with a mountain of whipped cream and an abundance of sweetener was deemed fine. Eating candy was bad, but eating a chocolate croissant was okay. Juice was bad, but juice with water or a glass of sweetened soy milk was good. In no case did a parent actually list the benefit of any of the products they preferred, but they were clear to outline what was bad about the candy, juice, and McDonald's—sugar and preservatives. No one identified the "healthier" options as including many of the same problems. Eating candy and going to McDonald's were considered markers of a family's class due to the food's association with unhealthiness. This judgment of class was more important than the actual nutritional value in the candy or McDonald's food. Turning one's nose up at McDonald's and other fast foods was one way that upper-middle-class parents could consciously separate themselves from working-class parents while at the same time position themselves as "good" parents.

Carmela (whose outlook on life seems more free-spirited than many of the other parents because of her dedication to child-centered direction in parenting) had definite ideas about what should be served on a playdate: "Always snacks! Vegetables, fruit, crackers, something organic. You try to do your best at a playdate. I would serve the best of the best at a playdate. Like now the best of the best is like Veggie Booty, you know [Veggie Pirate's Booty is a puffed corn snack with powdered cheese]. We try to do hummus, or carrots and cucumbers, fruit or you know, with a whole-foods–mindedness. Try to stay away from sugar although it always goes there anyway, so yeah, the healthiest snacks possible."

FIGURE 4.1. Kid-friendly packaging and advertising for Pirate's Booty snack.

When I conducted an extensive online comparison between tortilla chips, Cheetos, Pirate's Booty, and a few other snacks by going to
the manufacturers' websites, it soon became apparent how confusing
it can be to determine which were the healthiest snacks. I looked at the
ingredients for all snacks, compared vitamin values, and nutrient facts.
For example, while Cheetos and Veggie Pirate's Booty are both made
from cornmeal, the Pirate's Booty had less sodium. Yet neither had any
vegetables or vitamins. Therefore, since there was no nutritional value
to either, both would be considered junk food. Yet Pirate's Booty was
considered the "better choice" of snack food. If one compared baked
tortilla chips to Pringles fat-free potato chips, Pringles would come out
on top because of its lower fat content, yet parents did not want to serve
"chips." Somehow corn chips were seen as healthier than "chips." Both
tortilla chips and Pirate's Booty would not be considered "the healthiest snacks possible" if we looked strictly at nutritional value.[8] What this

Nutrition Facts

Pirate's Booty - Aged White Cheddar Puffs

Servings: 1	1 oz (about 36 pieces) ▼

Calories	195	Sodium	205 mg
Total Fat	10 g	Potassium	0 mg
Saturated	2 g	Total Carbs	23 g
Polyunsaturated	0 g	Dietary Fiber	2 g
Monounsaturated	0 g	Sugars	4 g
Trans	0 g	Protein	6 g
Cholesterol	0 mg		

Vitamin A	0%	Calcium	0%
Vitamin C	0%	Iron	8%

*Percent Daily Values are based on a 2000 calorie diet. Your daily values may be higher or lower depending on your calorie needs.

FIGURE 4.2. Nutrition facts for Pirate's Booty.

Nutrition Facts

Mission - Tortilla Triangles Chips

Servings: 1	28 g (28g ~ 10 chips) ▼

Calories	616	Sodium	221 mg
Total Fat	5 g	Potassium	1,623 mg
Saturated	2 g	Total Carbs	74 g
Polyunsaturated	1 g	Dietary Fiber	10 g
Monounsaturated	1 g	Sugars	18 g
Trans	0 g	Protein	45 g
Cholesterol	0 mg		

Vitamin A	165%	Calcium	10%
Vitamin C	115%	Iron	15%

*Percent Daily Values are based on a 2000 calorie diet. Your daily values may be higher or lower depending on your calorie needs.

FIGURE 4.3. Nutrition facts for Mission Tortilla Chips.

Nutrition Facts

Cheetos - ++ Cheetos Puff ++

Servings:	1	1 oz (28g/ About 13 pieces)	▼

Calories	60	Sodium	55 mg
Total Fat	0 g	Potassium	0 mg
Saturated	0 g	Total Carbs	0 g
Polyunsaturated	0 g	Dietary Fiber	2 g
Monounsaturated	0 g	Sugars	4 g
Trans	0 g	Protein	2 g
Cholesterol	0 mg		

Vitamin A	0%	Calcium	0%
Vitamin C	0%	Iron	0%

*Percent Daily Values are based on a 2000 calorie diet. Your daily values may be higher or lower depending on your calorie needs.

FIGURE 4.4. Nutrition facts for Cheetos Puffs.

means is that there really is not a meaningful difference between these various processed snacks; rather, there is a branding strategy at work. The bags of Pirate's Booty can be found in most health food stores, indicating immediately that there is some health value to them; moreover, the illustration on the bag is directed to children and includes the title "Veggie," which makes people believe that it is somehow a healthy alternative.[9] Parents like Carmela and Anna believed that they were making these objective choices of what is best for the kids, yet they are simply choosing certain items on the basis of branding and the class image that they are attempting to project to the parents who attend the playdate.

Parents have certain expectations when other parents are in charge of a playdate. Parents expect the host parents to keep the children safe by creating a private playspace in the home away from the public space of a park or sidewalk; they also expect the children to be dropped back home or picked up at an appropriate time, and fed if the time of day warrants a snack or meal. For many, these are the unwritten rules that parents should abide by, and if you are part of the same social class, these rules should be apparent. Anna described the unwritten rules about playdates, especially for members of the same social class: "I think it should be understood that the kids should be picked up before dinner if it is a drop-off playdate. I would expect that my kids be fed if they were there over lunch. I would hope that my child shows manners, which she does about 50 percent of the time. Definitely snacks and if it crosses a certain time then dinner or lunch. I would be surprised if my kids were not fed. I kinda feel like if the kid is on a playdate it is a special time, so they can eat whatever they want. I don't care if anybody were to feed my kid. . . . I don't want them smoking cigarettes with my kids, but soda and chips wouldn't bother me, although soda would surprise me if it was offered." Although Anna does not approve of soda on a playdate, she said that her family does drink soda on Saturdays as a treat. Ice cream and do-nuts, however, would be fine. She felt that the gentrified neighborhood she lives in, which is mostly white middle- to upper-middle-class, tends to be uptight about such food choices and stated that her house is not an organic house, so she understood that her choices when parents are over are different from when they are not. Anna is organic only when she is putting on a frontstage performance for guests, but not when living her life in the backstage. Again, Anna is consciously reifying what is expected of her class membership and will mask her backstage performance in order to maintain the relationships that are based on this membership.

Participants, regardless of socioeconomic status, tended to state that they offered healthy choices on playdates. Those who went out of their way to put out organic foods or "the best of the best" clearly suggested doing it for health reasons, but they are also putting on a performance. As one participant put it, doing so says to the other parents, "This is what I'm giving your children, right?" and "Is this what you're giving my children?" This performance of offering the healthiest option will be rewarded within the social group by either emotional reciprocity or social group status when the parents say to one another, "So-and-so has the best food at her playdates." For working-class parents, with one exception, this anxiety did not seem to exist. The one exception was the working-class mother who worked on behalf of the PLUs (People Like Us) as a yoga instructor and had been a vegetarian for years, so her outlook on foodways differed from the others. For middle- to upper-middle-class parents, however, who shared a PLU status, the anxiety around food came from worrying that they may be seen as not being a PLU and, therefore, have other parents speak badly of them or not get invited to subsequent playdates. This self-consciousness about class membership and social inclusion demonstrated how PLUs had little concern for the kids' actual nutrition, which fell low on the list of importance.

Carmela made a concerted effort, as she said, to do her "best" and present food that is "the best of the best." This frontstage performance that she is putting on for the other parents is what she determined connected her to the social group that she was interacting with at these playdates. But she maintained that it is distracting to have to think all the time about preparing for a playdate and conforming to other parents' expectations. Someone once told her, "If you think about cleaning your house every time you have playdates, you'll never have playdates." She concluded for herself that "nobody really lives this way, so if I'm gonna have someone over, I have needs and I have to have priorities. I edit. I don't mop the floor, but I'll clean the toilet. I don't clean the fridge, but I'll clean the kitchen." Carmela now minimizes the effort it takes to impress those parents whom she is entertaining at the playdate; she does still prepare for her performance, but without becoming as obsessed about it as she once had.

For Carmela, having a clean home communicated a potential class marker to those parents she was hosting. A clean home at all times communicated that her children were clean and neat (read properly raised), and that Carmela herself had time to clean the house (read as having enough leisure time and caring enough to clean). Having a clean house would possibly put parents at ease in allowing their kids to come over on their own, knowing the home was in order and not chaotic. Carmela was concerned with gaining the social capital necessary to foster a community of friends for her children and for herself.

The Consequence of Being in Charge

As discussed, for Elizabeth and most parents, a playdate will typically include a snack time. According to her, "If the playdate is in my house it's gonna be a healthy snack, there's going to be fruit involved, there might be yogurt. If it is lunch time I will make them a sandwich of some sort, or pasta. Or pizza or something like that."[10] She mentioned that her older daughter, on her own, writes out a program for the younger daughter's playdates for fun (no other parent mentioned their older children doing this), which included specified activities from one hour to the next, including snack time: "'We're going to have a puppet show and then we're going to have a dance performance.' . . . She really scripts it out. She gets excited about the playdates. . . . She sets the table. Part of it for me has been learning to be a hostess," since television is not on during the playdate. Part of this hostess role is feeding the children and parents a healthy snack at the appropriate time. If she knows that she will have three or four kids over to the house, she will make sure that she has three or four of the same yogurt in the house so that nobody feels left out if they didn't get one. She admits it costs money to have a playdate. However, when her daughters go to someone else's home, the choices are not necessarily always the same. For the younger daughter, Elizabeth typically stays at the playdate to see "who the parents are, who is in the house, and how they talk." Through surveillance Elizabeth is sizing up the class membership of the parents to ensure that her daughter is among PLUs, which provides Elizabeth with a certain comfort level. On the other hand, now that her older daughter is at an age where she can have drop-off playdates, Elizabeth says she just has to trust her daughter's choices since her daughter should now be able to decipher PLUs. One mother called her once to say that Elizabeth's older daughter said she couldn't have soda, but the other kids were being served soda, so she wanted to know whether she could give the soda to her daughter. After feeling like she was being put on the spot, Elizabeth asked the mother, "What's it that your kid can't do so I can pay you back?" Apparently she found out that the other mother is anti–Sponge Bob (a cartoon with mature content), so Elizabeth got the kid a pair of Sponge Bob pajamas as a nasty joke. From this action, it became apparent that Elizabeth wanted to assert her authority as the mother by letting the parent know that if she could go against her wishes in terms of what her daughter could consume, then Elizabeth could go against that mother's wishes and buy her kid Sponge Bob attire. Elizabeth could have told the mother that her daughter could not have the soda, but because the mother called Elizabeth in the presence of all the girls who were drinking soda, putting pressure on her to conform and let her child also take the soda, Elizabeth felt compelled to retaliate.

Elizabeth's authority was undermined again when her eldest daughter, who was nine years old, attended her first sleepover. The host father was sitting in the middle of the living room floor, watching an R-rated movie in the presence of the eight girls, the family guests. Elizabeth's daughter came home the next day and told her about the incident, adding that the movie had five curse words in it. Elizabeth said that her daughter was paying enough attention to the movie to realize it was inappropriate, so Elizabeth called the host mother because she felt close enough to the family to inquire. The mother said, "He's an idiot and he didn't want to get up and he thought they were not paying attention." The daughter has not slept over again, even though they are still good friends. Elizabeth felt comfortable with the parents and blames the dad for making a bad decision. Because these parents are PLUs, Elizabeth has not felt the need to completely disassociate her family from them, but the incident demonstrates that regardless of class membership, parents can do irresponsible things when children are around. This also shows that enclosing play in the private sphere might appear safer but can also create uncomfortable, and perhaps even unsafe, conditions, thereby undermining the point of enclosure.

This study shows how the social ritual of offering food to children while on a playdate reflects parents' perceptions of their own social selves in the context of a larger community. Classes of parents intentionally use this ritual to gain acceptance and feel included in their own social class, while other classes of parents do little to gain acceptance from others. While those who do little appear to be trying their best as parents, they remain excluded from total integration into middle- or upper-middle-class communities. Social class, therefore, is reproduced through the food selection by parents while on the playdate.

Another way of performing class is by adhering to playdate etiquette. Etiquette is the primary social class marker for Carmela. The one unwritten rule for Carmela on the playdate is that you should always bring something. "You don't come empty-handed. It's not rude, but it's always nicer to bring something. The kids definitely need to be provided food," she said. For her a bad playdate would mean an absence of what I call a social food space, namely, that there is no food being shared and consumed as part of the social relationships being created. The social food space that is created on a playdate equates to a good playdate for Carmela.[11] The playdate must satisfy the expectations of other parents. She also contends that sometimes other people's choices are simply not the ones she would make on a playdate, but because of her acceptance of people from various backgrounds, she feels that she has to be flexible.

Carmela said that she exposes her children to very wealthy families, in contrast to the family who lived upstairs from her. Carmela began to describe the family upstairs, with whom she had many playdates: "The neighbors were Hispanic and, you know, have no problem sticking their kids in front of the television and feeding them a lot of sugar, and there's a lot of Disney. I'm okay with that. The mother was conscientious. The mom felt she did her absolute best, and I felt that. I could feel that she really thought about her choices. They weren't my choices. I found her choices to be horrendous, actually, but there was love. We still do play-dates with them." Carmela's remark that "the neighbors were Hispanic and . . . have no problem sticking their kids in front of the television" demonstrates her endorsement of a blanket stereotype. In this case, tele-vision watching was a class marker, so her conflating being Latino/a with television watching illustrated how race and ethnicity can get wrapped up in people's perceptions of specific social classes. This creates further tension for parents as they begin to make decisions about whom to ap-proach for a playdate, and thus the self-selection and class reproduction cycle continues.

However, what was interesting about Carmela in particular is that, unlike many of the other parents with whom I spoke, she maintains a re-lationship with this particular neighbor and continues to have her child interact with the neighbor's children. When she spoke about her choices, however, a slightly patronizing tone arose. When asked whether or not she grew up with a lifestyle of no television, she said, "Not at all." When I asked her why she thinks that this choice is better than what she grew up with, she answered, "Because my choices are perfect," and then let out a big laugh. She continued, "Most of the choices I make to parent my kids are the right choices." Her mother told her that she did the best she could and felt a little guilty for not knowing more about healthy choices, in contrast to Carmela, who has chosen to rear her child "natu-rally." Carmela practices attachment parenting and natural birthing, and does not believe in vaccinations for her children. Attachment parenting for her meant breastfeeding her child until the child herself chose not to breastfeed any longer. She essentially followed the child's lead in all regards. Carmela's ideology is similar to what Sharon Hays described as "intensive mothering" in her 1997 book *The Cultural Contradictions of Motherhood*. Intensive mothering involves a child-centered perspective that is emotionally and labor-intensive, and childrearing is primarily if not wholly done by the mother. Hays also found that the unrealistic, self-imposed obligations required by this form of mothering are quite expensive. In order for a mother to tend to her children in this attached form, the mother would have to have ample time off to be with the child or have a job that is conducive to such a parenting style, and there would need to be significant income from a partner to allow for the mother to stay home to constantly be with the child. There is a lot of pressure on parents to adhere to certain parenting styles, many of them quite costly in terms of time, emotion, and finance.

"I'm not a big fan of nannies," Carmela said, "or raising your kids in the daycare system. I know that my choices are privileged choices. Bottle feeding, for instance, I don't believe in it. Whether I feel this person is a loving person, are they warm, . . . I'm willing to overlook almost everything. I'm very empathetic." This concerted effort to be constantly attentive to the child's needs could be argued as a form of subordination in that Carmela is now forfeiting many modern-day conveniences in order to ensure the privilege she deems important.

It was unclear from Carmela's comments whether she maintained the relationship with the Hispanic family because it was convenient to have playdates within the apartment building where she rented, felt sorry for the family and thus wanted to expose them to a "better" way of life, or had developed a meaningful relationship due to her openness to people unlike herself (perhaps all three). The contradiction between her words and actions indicates that, as for most mothers, personal moral standards or need for convenient childcare sometimes wins over one's class standards. Carmela recognized that the mother living above her reproduced family norms in a different way than she did. Carmela herself is reproducing family norms differently from her own mother, indicating a need to assert her own household position.[12]

For PLU mothers Carmela, Anna, and Elizabeth, there seemed to be certain acceptable fashions in childrearing, whether it is how to talk to a child, how to feed a child, or what to let the child watch while they are at a playdate. There are certain childrearing patterns that are fashionable, and then parents make the conscious decision to participate or not based on what is considered acceptable to their particular social group. For the working parents interviewed who did not organize playdates, there were no such anxieties about what children ate, how they were fed, or whether or not the children were allowed to watch television, which is how the middle- to upper-middle-class parents had grown up themselves. All classes of parents' social self became a reflection of the social community that they are engaged in, but for working-class parents, their social self was also a reflection of the community they were raised in.[13] Middle- to upper-middle-class parents worried about their front-stage performance, which mostly differed from their backstage, while working-class parents did not appear to worry as much about how they were perceived. The consequences of this are that middle- and upper-middle-class parents mediate all interactions to protect class status and social position and to benefit their children's integration with those of similar status and position, while working-class parents allow their children to mediate for themselves.

Discipline

Discipline seemed to be a topic that all parents could agree on in terms of what is expected behavior on a playdate and how a parent should handle an out-of-control child. Each participant interviewed agreed that children should be disciplined if they become violent, show disrespect to someone, or are "becoming unglued." There were no participants in this study, including the nannies, who said that they used spanking as way to discipline a child on a playdate.[14] Most agreed that some version of counting to a number (usually three) for a child to change their behavior, or time-outs, should be used. Some said that they took away choices or privileges from the child or redirected their attention in order to change behavior at a playdate. Others simply left the playdate with their child if the undesirable behavior continued.

While the topic of discipline seemed straightforward, it did involve some tension. Fathers tended to actively impose discipline in front of other parents, whereas mothers would await discipline from the other parent.[15] Parents, however, did not always agree with how other parents were disciplining or not disciplining their children, and often decided not to schedule any more playdates with them. Yet some parents, despite the poor behavior of children, continued to have playdates with certain families due to the close friendship they felt toward the parents.

Franco, the father of two who stated in an earlier chapter that he did hold playdates with his close family or friends despite how their children behave, felt that playdates are "more performance-oriented." He gave an example of how a child on a playdate could be doing something that one would never allow their own child to do. Franco said he would go over to his own son and let him know that he is not to behave that way in front of the other parent who isn't doing anything about the behavior at all. He believed that by modeling this behavior, he was ultimately going to change the behavior of both the parent and the child with whom they were having a playdate. He felt that with this performance he communicated to the other parent that they ought to be doing something and that in some way they were being judged. Whether or not this was actually effective, Franco believed wholeheartedly that it was appropriate discipline on a playdate because he was modeling the appropriate reaction.[16]

For Franco, staying on top of your child if they are being rude or not sharing is considered good discipline. He did not believe in directly disciplining someone else's child unless his child was in imminent danger. Having his child take a moment by redirecting or having a gentle talk with the child to indicate what behavior is acceptable and what is not, even in front of their guest or host, is Franco's preferred method of discipline.[17]

On the other hand, George, the father of a teenager and a college student, remembered distinctly how he reacted once on a playdate eleven years ago when he attempted to discipline his children using a harsh tone. He said that after saying something to the kids, he realized that he "sounded just like my father, and that's going to be about six months in therapy" for the kids later. George vowed never to speak to the kids that way in front of their friends again, and resorted instead to strategies that redirected the children's attention or simply cut the playdate short. However, this did not always work and caused friction with other parents.

For example, on one playdate, George's son, who was five at the time, lost at playing checkers and had a tantrum. The other father was trying to lecture George's son and said, "You've got to behave well or you won't be able to come back here." George said both he and his wife were present at the playdate. According to George, the father "went on and on and then we had to try to get him dressed because the playdate was clearly over," and George and his wife never repaired that relationship with the other parents. While George admits that his son was a lot more work than his daughter in terms of competitiveness and behavior, he realized that there is "a flavor of parent that thinks you can just reason with a child and as long as you feel good about it, the child will accept it, and it is true that there are children who will go along with that," but clearly his son was not one of those children. George's child did not necessarily listen to reason and reacted more emotionally. The success of playdates with the son was always tempered by how long the playdate went, meaning the longer the playdate, the more chance of having an unsuccessful playdate, although the particular tantrum, to which reference was made, happened right at the beginning, thus cutting short any possibility of success.

While the people with whom George tended to have playdates were part of the upper-middle-class PLU group, or as he put it, "interesting, well-educated, funny, and largely committed to the same things," he and his wife have had bad experiences with some parents. George, who is Asian American, recalled a playdate where his wife, who is white, had an unpleasant experience with a white woman who lived next door. He recounted the story: "Our kids were about six [and] she was allowing her son . . . her son started making jokes and saying, 'You look Chinese,' and manipulating his eyes in a kind of derisive way, and my wife said, 'Are you going to do something?' to the other mother, and the other mother said, 'Nah, it's just nothing, it doesn't mean anything,' and um, you know, the example we always use is if someone were calling our kid a kike, it would mean something, it's that kind of 'joking' that is more hurtful. . . . I hate this 'kids will be kids' thing because that's also the enabling of bullying. My wife was so furious about that, and the other woman was furious because my wife was interfering with her childrearing, which she was, and my wife was even more angry." In the end, and because they were neighbors, the two kids were friends, but the mothers did not interact in the same way, and the playdates all but ended.

George and Franco demonstrate what it is like to discipline and to be the recipient of discipline in front of other children's parents. While some in this study felt it better to take a child into another room, others felt it better to discipline a child in the moment.

Marzenna felt differently about discipline on a playdate. She did not like it when parents would discipline their children for "little things," although I would imagine that George's story would not necessarily qualify as "little." She said that playdates should be a time with as few rules as possible, due to the fact that she feels kids already have such rule-based lives: "It's all about listen, listen, listen, and do what you're told and that's what they hear 90 percent of the time, so I didn't want to set that kind of thing. . . . To me a playdate is about having a kid come over to play, it's not a lesson in socializing, even though I should probably consider it one." Few parents felt the same way as Marzenna, but the majority of parents determined that monitoring and supervision were required. As in the case of George's wife, where she interfered with the mothering of another, the parents who recalled similar stories felt that it was justified if a child was being disrespectful, violent, or insulting.

Elaine, the upper-middle-class Chinese mother from Canada, said that if there is violence, then the parents should step in no matter what. She said her son was on a playdate at a park when the other boy began to choke him. He also started to tease him, and Elaine's son could not stand up to him (he was about five at the time). She said the parents of the boy witnessed what was happening but never said anything. The following morning, the mother called to ask Elaine whether she would pick up her son from school. Elaine said, "Well, my son was really upset about what happened yesterday, so I'll have to see if he is okay with that." The son said it would be okay and so she picked the boy up and dropped him off at his home, but after that, Elaine stated, the parents avoided another playdate, although she still sees them in the schoolyard. In this case, Elaine, like George's wife, felt that the parents should have intervened. She awaited the expected parental performance, especially given their class similarities. She was disappointed that the mother felt no need to intervene, which debunks the idea that PLUs are truly PLUs, though there may have been something else at play in this interaction. I asked Elaine whether race could have been a factor. Elaine is Chinese Canadian, but said she did not feel that this inaction on the part of the parent, who is white, could be attributed to race. What this demonstrates is that sometimes, regardless of similarities in class, some parents just have a different way of disciplining (or not) their children. At times, the people like us come to be people unlike us in other ways.

If a parent does not intervene when their own child has violated the unwritten rules of a playdate, it tends to result in a severed relationship. The frontstage performance of intervention is considered high-stakes at a playdate. But the violations vary in seriousness. If the unwritten rule is to provide snacks and a parent does not do so, then it is more likely that a parent will forgive the host family and simply pack snacks for their own child the next time they arrange a playdate. Similarly, if two kids just do not get along, as was the case with Anna's daughter and her friend's child, but the parents have a close relationship, the play-dates may continue, but perhaps with longer breaks in between. In other words, they may hold a playdate every few months instead of weekly. However, if a child is being mocked or violated in any way, this could end any prior friendship for good.

While class is primarily used as a selection tool for playdates, at the end of the day, parents individually determine just how far they will allow a "bad" playdate to continue if discipline is not employed. Class reproduction is cultivated through this forced playdate as parents sacrifice their children's happiness on a playdate in the same way that certain foods are present or a house is clean, because one parent is seeking some form of acceptance from the other parent. Again, the frontstage performance and its acceptance by the audience are of utmost importance, due in large part to perceived or real future gain. This acceptance, in some cases, leads to job opportunities or future social engagements that are seen somehow as beneficial. Some families will continue to allow the children to socialize with little parental socialization, while others may continue to attend playdates as before because of some more beneficial social or cultural capital gain. If a parent recognizes the potential benefit to continuing a playdate gone bad, they are more likely to allow the playdate to continue regardless of whether the child is happy with the playdate partner. Finally, other parents will completely sever ties altogether, regardless of PLU status.

5

The Birthday Party

A Hyper-Playdate

"I want to have my birthday party at a bowling alley, just like Eva," my son pleaded nine months before his actual birthday. "I changed my mind. I want to have my birthday at Bounce U like Jonathan," he told me three months later. By July it was, "Mommy, can I have a Ninja party?" and then by August, after learning how to use a fishing rod, he asked, "Can I go on a real boat and have a fishing party for my birthday?" Here I was thinking that I am a month away from his sixth birthday, which happens to fall on the day that everyone sighs at when I say it—September 11.

When did birthdays become so extravagant? I wondered. The parents of my son's school friends were spending upwards of six hundred dollars for a birthday party to which nearly the whole class was invited. Six hundred dollars? I thought to myself. Really? For a party the kids won't even remember? Two weeks from his birthday and I finally settled on asking my son's tae kwon do teacher to help pull together a Ninja party. He was game—to the tune of $250 for up to twenty kids. That seemed like the best deal I could find that fit my son's interests. I still had to provide food, drinks, and goodie bags (the ultimate waste of money, although the kids love them). I realized that I was doing this party only because my son had seen what other kids had done for their birthday parties, a similar pressure that parents feel. Having completed kindergarten and been invited to some lavish birthday parties, my son campaigned for me to give him an official event. Settled, Ninja party for ten on September 11.

The children's birthday parties I have attended in the last few years have brought laughter and smiles, tears, twisted ankles, a hospital trip for a split forehead that required stitches, and hurt feelings because a child did not get a chance to sit beside the birthday kid for the group picture. These experiences sounded all too familiar given the several playdates I had attended and those that had been recalled for me by participants for this book. I call the birthday party a "hyper-playdate" because the birthday party experience has many of the same qualities of a play-date, only more pronounced.[1] For example, the birthday parties of the upper-middle-class families that I spoke to tend to be at a private or enclosed location that is rented for a specified amount of time, usually two to three hours. There is almost always a prepared activity that will take place: a gymnastics class, dance-along, learning about live animals and petting them, listening to songs that are played by a musician, and for the even more intellectually curious, a man who comes dressed as Abraham Lincoln and reads to the children. There are also the standard games such as pin the tail on the donkey, the piñata, the balloon toss, or the arts and crafts table, but these are falling out of fashion with some of the upper-middle-class parents who were interviewed for this book.[2] Instead, these parents are spending large amounts of money to outsource one or more parental responsibilities to an even lower-wage workforce to impress other parents or colleagues with a commercial rented space that can accommodate everyone in the child's class and their families. The April 6, 2015, *New Yorker* cover parodied the growing phenomenon. On this cover, children line up like patrons at an exclusive nightclub, gifts in hand. A large "Happy Birthday" banner and a room filled with balloons are visible in the background just beyond the line. The children in line appear to behave more like status-obsessed upper-class adults than overexcited children: two are engrossed in reading their smartphones and another is holding up her present, snootily bragging about it to others, who are listening raptly. Meanwhile, a well-muscled, imposing bouncer stands in front of them all, guarding the entrance to the party behind a velvet rope.

FIGURE 5.1. *New Yorker* cover from April 6, 2015.

Although meant to be humorous, the *New Yorker* cover exemplifies the high stakes for children's birthday parties in contemporary society. The birthday party has become an intensified playdate within a privatized commons. Although there is restricted space in New York City homes, which could be a reason for such outsourcing, I found that participants living in more suburban areas such as Long Island also outsourced birthday parties. As in a playdate, there is always food, although this is played down for some birthday parties. For preschoolers, parents may put out bagels and lox, cream cheese, and organic fresh fruit, usually by kindergarten the kids eat pizza, soda/juice, and birthday cake or the more trendy cupcakes. The party also takes on features of the playdate because instead of dropping their children off to a party, parents often stay and drink coffee or eat alongside the children, albeit at a different table or standing up, or in a different room with different food from the children once the kids are older. The playdate is emulated in the parents' space, since this is when future playdates can be planned or parents engage in social/professional networking. Another similarity to the playdate is that in a party, the host parents spend money to impress the other families, but even more money is spent on a party, since there is often an outside venue to rent, with more children to accommodate. The consumption aspect of birthday parties can be seen in the money that is spent on them, the way they are commodified using leisure playspaces in and around New York City, and how some parents categorize some parties as "better" than others. There is also a gendered aspect to these parties, whereby mothers are typically the ones who organize them and fathers of the guest children attend to spend time with their children, since many are working full-time out of the home during weekdays.[3]

According to Alison J. Clarke, a social anthropologist who wrote about the negotiation of birthday parties in North London, birthday parties are a complex interaction of identities, economics, and gender.[4] Her analysis of ethnographies on birthday parties illustrates the various ways that birthday parties become a commercialized social ritual as opposed to what she suggests used to be more of a community gathering. Clarke suggests that the birthday party can be seen as having a "snowball effect" on how to arrange a party, how to buy appropriate gifts, and when to attend a party or not. Mothers in Clarke's book, who tended to plan the parties or were the first in their social group or class to plan a birthday party, set the standard for other mothers. In this way, according to Clarke, mothers are now managing what has become a reciprocal event. A negotiated consensus about mothering takes place, in which mothers implicitly understand that they must host parties that are equally lavish as the ones their children attend. Clarke also argues, as I do in this book, that the "non-economic world of children" transforms into an economic one, which the children will then reproduce on some level as they begin to request specific birthday themes, playspaces to hold the party, or foods.[5] As Clarke discusses, this expectation due to children's increasing agency as they grow older will eventually supersede the woman's role as mother and destabilizes her maternal identity. While this direct identity crisis is not analyzed in this book, since it did not show up in the data, there is a clear sense that social and class reproduction is happening at birthday parties. This chapter will build on Clarke's work to determine how social reproduction is cultivated through the birthday party. Participants' expenditure of money and decisions on what constitutes "good food" become part of the reproduction that Clarke speaks of in her research. In addition, it is clear that regardless of the child's needs, mothers want to perform for their "circle of friends."

The extravaganza of these hyper-playdates was detailed by most participants as something they organize to ensure that children keep up with those in their class. Caroline, whom I had met at the virtual café, spent over $3,000 for her four-year-old's birthday party and would be holding a party at Elite this year in Soho, where you can have a gymnastics party for around $800. At these parties, Caroline said, she invited parents whom she and her husband would like to see, along with the children in her daughter's classroom. They also hired additional babysitters to keep the children under control even though the parents would be present and the facility that she is paying hundreds of dollars to also has staff on hand. Caroline also makes sure that there is wine for afternoon parties for the parents as well as adult food, not pizza. Even the pizza for kids is ordered from a high-end restaurant that makes thin-crust pizza and advertises itself as healthier than other pizza places. Her girls always have a birthday party with friends and then a birthday day, a family birthday celebration at home on the actual date of the birthday, which most parents admit that they do.

After attending several birthdays over the last several years with her children, Caroline said that she had seen all types of birthday parties and that most of them are lavish. She said that parents typically know someone at restaurants where they can rent a space for their children and bring in entertainment like a puppet show and magicians, a feature that is not available to the general public. Some parties are held in people's large Manhattan lofts where they can accommodate thirty children. During the summer, parents typically do not invite the whole class, but as Caroline states, "There's pressure to invite everyone in order to be polite. . . . But it is important that the kids don't talk about the party because other kids get their feelings hurt." The teachers Melanie and Linda said the same. When children are left out of party invitations, they said, it is "traumatic." They see the child in class, when everyone else is discussing it, become sad and sometimes the child will express how left out they feel. The hyper-playdate morphs from a gender-neutral event to either a "girls only" or "boys only" party once the children turn six, according to a few parents. According to one of the Long Island mothers who was interviewed, by age six, parents want to simplify the birthday party experience due to logistics and finances. In addition, most parents have established their social network by the time their children reach this age, so impressing an entire class worth of parents becomes less necessary. This is sometimes at the direction of the children, but mostly it is a way for parents to cut the invitee list in half, thus cutting costs. So eventually children are excluded from the hyper-playdate based on gender, but by that point, they do not feel left out as they may have during the co-ed parties.

Lauren is a mother of Jewish descent who is raising a five-year-old and an almost-seven-year-old. She works part-time, has a master's degree in education, rents an apartment in a brownstone building in Carroll Gardens, Brooklyn, and has a family income of over $200,000, mostly stemming from her husband's work. Lauren's experience with birthday parties exemplifies the differences between economic classes. In her words, "The cultural/economic differences were made clear when one of the Latino boys in my younger son's class had a school birthday party with Domino's pizzas and Coke served in large plastic straw cups [Big Gulp size] that advertised Dominos. . . . Many of the middle-class parents [regardless of race or ethnicity] were uncomfortable with this party and said as much on the playground for days afterward. It became a 'thing.' I know it was surely more expensive than the vegan cupcakes we baked." What Lauren is suggesting is that quality food does not have to cost a lot; therefore, those who are economically less advantaged than her should be able to provide healthier options to the children at parties.[6]

Lauren worried that her younger son, who was already on the cusp of being at risk for obesity in his vegan household, would like the soda and pizza, which she says he never had before (or at least, not that she knows of). She said that many of the parents even spoke to the teacher about serving soda to the children during class hours, especially in the age of shows like *Jamie Oliver's Food Revolution*.[7] Lauren continued, regarding her son switching schools, "The population at [public school 1] is simply not the same as [public school 2]; candy is regularly sent home in class party goodie bags, and when parents are asked to contribute 'healthy' snacks for the class, the interpretation of healthy is pretty wide." This interpretation meant that some parents thought that cookies and candies were considered healthy snacks (or simply what kids wanted), while others believed that fruits and vegetables were the better choice. Both the goodie bags and the candy/cookies were indications of class value judgment. If the goodie bags were plastic containing plastic toys, the class implication was significantly different than a brown paper bag that can be recycled or a cotton designer bag, which displayed a higher status. Choice also became an issue for many parents when it came to drinks. Most parents preferred water, but others were fine with soda or juice "cocktails" with added sugar or corn syrup instead of 100 percent juice. These differences were not simply about food or gift choices, but rather what these choices represented—a difference in socioeconomic class. The question remains, what creates this anxiety among parents? And if a parent is already privileged, why should it matter what is offered at a party?

Pointing out the differences between classes based on food was a common topic for participants in this study. Caroline said that she prefers not to get a goodie bag full of "junk" and candy, and at her parties, she opts to give out items like a cupcake holder or a set of crayons and a real-sized coloring book or a big box of chalk. Lorena, who would be considered to be in a lower economic bracket compared to Caroline, said that in East Harlem she used to take her children to McDonald's for birthday parties since that was easier for winter birthdays than going outdoors to a park, but Emily in Brooklyn, who is in a higher economic bracket although only by $25,000, stated that birthday parties such as these are not the types of parties she enjoys and would probably not let her kids go due to the quality of food, implying that the low-quality food equates to a party fit for only "certain types" of people, with whom her children cannot socialize. Emily also plans for her daughter's winter birthday party and admitted that it costs more because she cannot simply go to the playground to have a party, and since the homes in New York are mostly small, a party at home is not an option either. She has held birthday parties at indoor spaces that she rents for her only child, but has also been to quite a few parties that have made her uncomfortable. Emily went on to discuss the birthday parties that take place at Chuck E. Cheese's in the Atlantic Center Mall in Brooklyn, a space that is generally frequented by black and brown families and disparaged by upper-middle-class white parents, although on certain days you can find a large Orthodox Jewish population. She stated that the family that organized the party is a "hard-luck family and [I] thought I was going to be the only one there [meaning the only one of her class] because the kids were new to the school and I wanted to support the parent. . . . I paid to help defray the costs [of the party]. I don't care about that. I had never been to Chuck E. Cheese and have tried to avoid it at all costs. It was kids everywhere and I swear I saved a kid from dying." Emily went on to explain how the chaos on the slide caused one kid to be on top of another and it was dangerous enough that Emily had to grab a girl who was being smothered by five other children. Emily's daughter came to her soon after with blood coming out of her nose and then told her that some kid had kicked her in the nose. Emily continued, "That's when I was like, . . . these are not my people. . . . The only drink available was soda, and the food was nothing that I would ever feed her [her daughter]. . . . It was like being in a kiddie casino," referring to the tokens received at games and the coins that children accumulate for prizes toward the end of the day. "We are never going back to Chuck E. Cheese." In this case, by stating, "these are not my people," Emily is referring to class. Specific values are seen as accepted by one class of people, in this case what Emily referred to as lower- (read working-) class, and rejected by other classes, what Emily considered middle-class. The anxiety around this stems from a safety issue that Emily witnessed with the chaos at the party, along with a health concern regarding the food.

Class distinction was vital to parents such as Emily, whose kids needed to be in appropriate settings for their social class at all times. The policing of Chuck E. Cheese's and McDonald's by the upper-middle-class parents in this study was interesting due to the fact that although they are enclosed spaces, they are seen as too chaotic and child-centered in the sense that the child may "choose" to actually eat or drink whatever they wanted. Parents were active participants in the monitoring of behavior even at a time that is supposed to be all about the kids.

While these apparent class differences between parents seemed common among participants, there were other parents making over $250,000 a year who opted not to hold extravagant parties. Some parties were held at the home of the child with traditional kids' games; there were dance parties with glow lights that kids wore on their fingers as they danced; there were dress-up parties. Children were offered pasta as a meal option and candy/cake as a treat afterwards with juice and sometimes soda. These parties did not seem to be too different from the Chuck E. Cheese's parties except for the fact that they were not held at Chuck E. Cheese's. The home parties seemed more like a playdate with a handful of children and organized activities and were not frowned upon as were the parties at Chuck E. Cheese's. It should be noted that none of the working-class parents mentioned Chuck E. Cheese's as a venue where they held parties. This class value judgment was solely from the perspective of those in the middle to upper-middle class.

Maria from Manhattan stated that for her two children, it is important that both the parents and the kids make decisions about whom to invite to their birthday parties. Anna, who could afford any type of party she chose, felt the same. Anna said that she asked her older daughter to make up a list for her birthday party. Then Anna laughed and said, "I completely edit the list," similar to the way playdates are curated by parents. Her daughter tended to include only the girls in her class, but as Anna put it, "there are certain people in our life that I cannot exclude, and so I invite them." These "certain people" were children of longtime friends of Anna's or her business partners' children. Although Anna will add to her daughter's list, she then cuts it down to twelve children maximum (although only around eight ever show up) and feels horrible because she understands that some kids will feel left out. She mentioned one child who has never been invited and her mother had been telling people that she is upset about it, but Anna defended her choice by stating, "My daughter has never talked about her. . . . Life's hard and you're not always going to be included and it's not about me being like choosing who is on her A list, it's just like not realistic." In all of the interviews, no fathers ever discussed the birthday party as something that they took care of. It was typically the wife who organized it. In addition, fathers only heard about the feelings of excluded families through the wife's re-telling of playground stories.

Anna said she sees no advantage to having a large birthday party. She thinks it is great if a parent feels compelled to invite the whole class, but feels that attending a large party "is really just not that important." At Anna's younger daughter's birthday parties, there were mostly kids whom Anna wanted to invite, since her daughter does not yet have many friends in pre-K that she can identify. At the end of it all Anna debated whether or not playdates or birthday parties were at all for the kids or just for the parents. She felt that the smaller party was more meaningful to the child than a larger one.

Elizabeth, who lives on Long Island, talked about a birthday party that she held at Sesame Place that accommodated thirty people for over two thousand dollars. She said that at larger birthday parties the kids end up crying or becoming overstimulated, yet she still did them in order to "please" her child. She also did a party once at the American Girl doll store in Manhattan with twenty-four people at forty dollars per person. This party cost around a thousand dollars, and she again said that the children end up overstimulated, but happy. Several parents implied to me that it is the memory of the lavish event that seems to bring happiness to both parent and child, regardless of the immediate chaos at the time. Elizabeth had gone to even larger birthday parties where parents had talent shows in a rented big top. The kids all came prepared to put on a show or display some talent. Elizabeth felt that the disadvantages to holding such a large party were that the kids were often overwhelmed and didn't feel connected to one another. She also noticed that dads tended to exchange business cards and network with one another, so it made sense for some parents to hold such large events.[8] Elizabeth alludes to the fact that the birthday party experience is more about the parents than the children, since she realizes that the kids are not really forming strong bonds with one another at the party and are overwhelmed by the event, yet the parents continue to hold large parties and even begin to network for business resources. Therefore, it becomes important for middle- and upper-middle-class parents who are seemingly privileged to keep up with one another, since important relationships may be formed for later networking opportunities that may eventually benefit their children's social network.

Unlike Elizabeth and her friends on Long Island, Erin said she talked about the birthday party all year with her daughter and made sure to tell her that it had to be smaller this year since it was always at home and too many people had been invited in previous years. Erin and her husband held a craft party once, but tried to limit the number of kids. The most she has spent on a party so far is around four hundred dollars. Erin stated that there are "no advantages to big parties. . . . They're horrible, . . . so much anticipatory energy and excitement. . . . There's no connecting with any of these kids. . . . I hate them [big parties]. Went to one with forty kids in the home in a brownstone. It was insanity and then there were forty presents." I asked whether at parties with so many gifts, kids still open them in front of the guests, as I had remembered it and as participants recalled from their youth. Erin said, "They no longer open presents in front of guests. . . . It is so grotesque. . . . I feel disappointed about it." Other friends of hers have resorted to just making a personal cake, getting balloons, and sitting with their family for a little party. Sharing Elizabeth's misgivings about larger parties, Erin felt that the smaller family party is a better option for birthdays since it is more personal and meaningful, not a contrived event with meaningless connections.

Regardless of the type of party, parents would initially cite the party as something they wanted to do for their child to make the child happy, but as we dug deeper, they all agreed that it was the parents who ended up enjoying the fact that they were able to provide their child with an event that they believed would be memorable, memorable in a way that conveys privileges and status to the child that they will likely believe they deserve, even if the children at the party were overwhelmed and crying.

Betsy's daughter, who is five and a half years old, only has home parties. Betsy is divorced, forty-three years old, and raising her daughter on $25,000 a year in the East Village while she works part-time as an actress and entertainer. In addition to her $25,000, she receives $2,000 from family members per month in order to support her daughter while she works to complete her associate's degree.

It was eighty-five degrees and humid outside the community college in Manhattan where we met. Betsy showed up for the interview even though she was recently separated from her husband and was now dealing with the death of her boyfriend in an accident a week earlier. She became more outgoing and jovial as we discussed birthday parties, since much of her work is centered around being an entertainer for children's parties.

Betsy claimed that in general East Village parties are unstructured, unlike those held in more affluent neighborhoods such as the Upper

East Side or Tribeca. One of the more crazy parties she discussed from her work was when a rumor spread at a crowded children's party that one of the kids pooped on the floor while all of the kids were running around. She stated that both the parents and the kids were buzzing, saying, "Oh my god, someone pooped all over the floor" and she could not believe how quickly the rumor had spread. Kids were screaming, parents were rushing after their children to make sure they did not step in it. People appeared disgusted, and everyone cleared the floor. After the staff came to inspect the "poop" disaster, it turned out just to be chocolate cake. This was the type of party that she said simply got out of control and where everyone seemed overwhelmed.

Given Betsy's experiences as a birthday party host and her economic bracket, I wondered whether she had ever been to a Chuck E. Cheese's birthday party, but she said no. She then said that she has been to the franchise, but not for a party and not in New York. She said it is not popular with the kids in Manhattan since the closest one is in Brooklyn (although there actually is one in Harlem that perhaps she was unaware of). Betsy went on, "I can never eat there because the food looks like it's been under a heat lamp for five hours, and the noise." Her rationale, though, was that it is not easy to get to from Manhattan, so her circle did not usually go to Chuck E. Cheese's. By "circle," she meant other artists in the East Village and some more affluent parents that she may work for on the Upper East Side. It appeared at this point that the Chuck E. Cheese's option really had little to do with income and more to do with perceived class status as well as location.

Betsy worked as a host for an Upper East Side indoor space that held classes for children and birthday parties. She said it could cost anywhere from $750 up, including pizza, cake, the room, and a host for two hours to hold a birthday party at this venue. She said that while some parents might participate with the children if they were very young (one year old), many parents would be eating and drinking wine in a room next door while the kids played with the party host. In this adjacent room, Betsy said, parents were not only making small talk but networking. In a man's voice, she mimics a conversation between two men: "Oh, you work at so and so. . . . Oh and you work at so and so, we should get together . . ." She stated that at her venue it was much more high-powered; mostly the dads or couples would show up for the reason given earlier: that the father is typically working during the weekdays.

This was quite different from what Betsy knew growing up. She remembered that at her birthday parties she was allowed to invite the same number of kids as the age she was turning. When she turned eight, for example, she was allowed to invite eight friends to the party. She also remembered the parties being held in the home and not at another venue. From her experience as a birthday party host, she found that the smaller parties were "much sweeter and calmer," not overwhelming like the larger parties. She also noted that the families tended to be more participatory and that "there is a more gentle energy" than the larger parties.

"There's usually a flavor that happens," she said. "Sometimes it's like, this party is for the parents, it's not for the kids at all, and then the reverse is true sometimes. . . . I love the ones that are for the kids. The grownups get nourishment also." As for the larger parties, Betsy noticed a huge difference in the way the parents approached the birthday party: "I think there is a certain level of nervousness about impressing the other parents that happens. There was one party where I was like, 'Jesus God, this has turned into like a wedding and just so tense and everything has to be perfect.' It's a one-year-old's birthday party, I mean it can be sweet, but not be a big deal. I mean it is a big deal, but not a big deal where every piece of tape has to be [perfect]." So there's a nervousness about the preparation that she takes note of to determine whether the party is really about impressing parents rather than the birthday child. When I asked her whether this nervousness impacted her work as a host, she claimed that it did, "because you are trying to deal with the kids and so there is a judgment and the parents are all in the other room while the kids are running around." She felt that if the kids were not returned to the parents happy and not overwhelmed and crying, she would have a complaint filed against her.

Betsy does see a birthday party as different from a playdate, but says the interaction of the parents is the same: they are off networking and building relationships while the kids are on their own. The one difference Betsy noted is that at a birthday party, parents have opportunities to interact with more people and therefore do not need to feel stifled by having to try to find something to talk about with only one other person, as in the case of a playdate in the home. In this sense, then, the larger birthday party is a hyper-playdate: parents are continuing to socialize and network along class lines, or as Betsy put it, "within their small circle," and the kids themselves are expected to be the benefactors of a selected interaction that has been facilitated by the parents.[9]

The consumption of birthday parties and expectations of modern mothers have created a commercialized event that requires sophisticated gift giving, complex management, and, for some, a negotiation over whom to invite. There are dedicated blogs on the Internet for moms who wish to learn how to make their child's favorite character cakes, where to buy props, order bouncy houses (the inflatable jungle gyms

FIGURE 5.2. Online party package service.

FIGURE 5.3. Sesame Place: Birthday packages offer character dining, party favors, and private cabanas for an additional price.

FIGURE 5.4. American Girl offers party packages. Birthday parties typically cost forty dollars per person, with additional costs depending on the type of package, including doll accessories that are purchased for children to take home.

that kids can jump around on), and gift bag ideas. These same blogs also offer detailed planning so parents do not need to do the heavy lifting, with prices beginning at eighty-five dollars.[10]

The social ritual of the birthday party, for participants in this study, function to separate middle-class children from working-class children. The People Like Us phenomenon creates value judgments that are quickly disseminated to children through this social ritual. The birthday party is not necessarily entirely for the child, although many attempt to portray the party as being about the birthday child. It is also used as a marker of class status among parental peers that may benefit the child as they age. While the birthday party does not stem from a moral panic, there is certainly a panic of sorts, if we apply Clarke's analysis of the commercialization of birthday parties. The panic stems from a need to maintain the mother's identity and role in the community. This angst among mothers appears to stem from the presentation of self (or family in this case). The birthday party becomes a display of economic advantage and thus class advantage. By holding elaborate festivities for young children, parents are able to demonstrate their affluence, their sense of quality and quantity, their class worth. If a mother can put on an event that is considered "playground-worthy," her children will be considered worthy of holding playdates with, or their parents considered worthy of getting to know better.[11] This angst creates a competition among groups of parents, thereby producing even more elaborate birthday parties. This implicit competition challenges their ability to woo other parents of their same class. It is this hyper-playdate that drives the economic market for birthday parties and the social reproduction of the upper-middle class.

Conclusion

As Simple as Child's Play

Playdates are a way for moms to not have to be one-on-one
with their kids, especially more stay-at-home moms, so they
can have that . . . socialization and, you know, they don't feel
guilty because their kids are still playing and having fun together. . . . You don't want to be stuck in the house by yourself. Getting out is important to keep your sanity and, you
know, you get ideas from each other, and just sometimes you
need to talk to someone else about maybe what's going on
inside your house or what's going on with your kid. . . . It's
important to not be stuck up in your own little world.
—Beatrice, twenty-nine, director of a private learning center
in Manhattan

Parents have a hard job keeping their children entertained, molding
them into decent citizens, and protecting them from harm. Playdates
have become one resource that parents utilize in order to do all of these
things and more. Playdates derive from dates, specific meetings between
two or more people, and represent a concentrated time to socialize for
children, but more so for parents, especially when children are younger.
It is through the playdate that parents find comfort in their own parenting skills, network among their peers (parents who are like them),
and expose their children to a class of people that parents deem socially
appropriate. Yes, a child also does get to build a more personal relationship with another child, but do the benefits of this "private date"
outweigh those of simple play? And to whose benefit is the playdate? Is

it any safer to have a playdate? Do playdates actually expose children to the range of people they might meet if you were to just send them out to play, or is the playdate simply a way for parents to attempt to create a sanitary version of play with particular groups of children? The answers to these questions depend on whom you ask.

In this study, I have been able to unveil some of the ways various parents, nannies, and educators use and discuss playdates as a tool to socialize children and to network among themselves. While some classes of adults seem to think playdates do indeed benefit their child or charge in some way, others find the playdate to be a perverse way of structuring play between children that is not really about the children but about creating a community among the adults.

Logistics of Raising Children in New York

New York being a densely populated urban space, it is not surprising that parents are conscious of the pervasive speed at which they live their daily lives. This speed creates not only a consciousness of having to schedule every detail of the daily routine, but also a sense of competition for scarce resources, including capital. Certain classes of parents acknowledge that they are the facilitators of how and with whom their children play due to their fears of living in a city that has had a reputation for being a fast and dangerous place to live. These parents favor the playdate as a privatized commons. Other parents maintain that children ought to figure out whom they want to play with by interacting with other children in their neighborhoods; these parents favor free, traditional, informal play. With the more formal playdate, details need to be taken care of, such as the location and time of the playdate, who is invited, and what is acceptable on the playdate as entertainment and as food. It is this formality that distinguishes the playdate from play. Playdates require far more negotiation, but with potentially higher stakes that include pleasing both children and parents in order to ensure future playdate encounters in the hopes of garnering social and cultural capital.

The People Like Us rhetoric sanitizes play in such a way that it creates exclusionary models of play. Parents who stay at home with their children and engage in frequent playdates demonstrated that they tend to exclude full-time working parents, typically mothers, from playdates due to the timing of playdates during the workweek. Parents sometimes, but not often, will arrange playdates with nannies or other childcare providers, but tend to stick with other parents for playdates. Fathers typically find other fathers who are at home with their kids and who have flexible hours during the workweek. Nannies tend to hold playdates only with other nannies, because they feel comfortable with those at their own class level. There are not too many gender divides when it comes to playdates; instead, parents are mostly excluded based on employment during the workweek. Lastly, race was an obvious criterion for exclusion. While parents attempted to recall the one mother or father of color with whom they would hold a playdate, such playdates seemed to be infrequent compared to playdates with parents of the same race. Parents of color seemed less likely to see the playdate as affecting their children's life chances.

Food and discipline also became criteria by which parents were judged. Regardless of the judgment going on between parents, at the end of many interviews and conversations about playdates, parents, especially mothers, felt that they were building community with other parents like themselves, thereby reproducing class. The pressure to "fit in" to a desirable group of parents was amplified in the birthday party celebrations (or hyper-playdates) that ranged from a party at the house to parties costing thousands of dollars. The commodification of play and celebration took on a whole new dimension when it came to birthday parties, but it is this precise event that solidified the demonstration of a person's social class position. For some families, children became an appendage to the parents' desire to fit in.

It is not all bad, though. Parents have a tough job, and it is easy to feel alienated as a parent with young children. Parents spend years accommodating the needs of other little beings while they mostly repress their own desires. At the end of the day, parents wanted to feel that they could communicate their fears to another person who shared their position as a parent. This need typically waned after the second child was born, but was still part of the connectedness that parents needed to feel as part of a society. An important issue that arises from the exclusion that takes place in the construction of the playdate experience is that parents are actively creating a sanitized version of social realities while contributing to the inequalities that already exist in society.

Inequality

"Who cares? It's just a playdate! Why are you making a big deal about this?" This is a typical statement that I hear when I speak casually about the topic of this book. I understand the defensiveness that this topic brings out among parents and nonparents alike. On the surface it may seem like a frivolous topic. After all, parents like to socialize and children like to play, so what is so hard to understand about that? My hope for this book is to shed light on how play has been transformed over generations and to analyze how we think of play and its ultimate purpose.

By interviewing parents, childcare providers, and educators, I have come to learn that, as a society, we find ways to re-create social class in something as simple as child's play. When statistics continue to indicate that white men dominate Fortune 500 companies—and the boardroom in most organizations, for that matter—how do childhood experiences play a role in this reproduction of "leaders" and "followers"? Certainly with parental anxieties there is a substantial amount of conformity, which is potentially how the playdate became such a popularized term, but it is more than that. Playdates provide networking opportunities that parents seek in order to "get ahead" and "belong." Many of us lay folks know that there are social circles, but how are social circles created beyond just the wealth one has accumulated? This book has shown how among certain groups of people something as simple as crafting playdates to exclude other groups of people is one way that parents begin the practice of creating a social circle. As parents, we are re-creating what we see in the boardroom. We redefine play to indicate how some people are acceptable and some are not, but more so what we are doing is not even allowing our children to figure out on their own what is acceptable or not. We are crafting the social circle in a more hands-on manner in response to not only perceived fears, but competition beginning in schools and continuing all the way to the workplace. Some commentators posit that if we simply place diverse classes and races of people under one roof, resources will be shared.[1] This study shows that this is simply not true. In New York City, there is a lot of diversity in concentrated areas. Most of the participants have children who are enrolled in the public school system, some with free lunch programs, meaning that there are a substantial number of children who qualify economically for the free lunch program at school. Despite the diversity of class and race in the public school system and despite the fact that most of these participants live in residentially diverse neighborhoods, upper-middle-class families continue to create private spaces through the playdate. They are able to exclude groups of people and reproduce their own racial and class advantages without being physically segregated. The quality and quantity of interactions with PLUs are not impacted by their close proximity to a range of people.

Upper-middle-class families nurture the norms set by their class through the lessons and organizational rules of playdates, while working-class families allow for more spontaneous interactions. Upper-middle-class families actively create situations to alleviate their anxieties about how social their children will be among certain types of people, while working-class families have more faith that their children will figure it out through practical experience. Inequality does begin somewhere, and this part of our socialization begins very early on. Playdates and birthday parties are just two of the earliest crafted encounters that parents are utilizing in order to socialize their children into certain circles for capital gain.

Perhaps children themselves know how to combat inequality. If we listen to the parents in this book and hear how their children want to play with certain people, in spite of the fact that parents continue to re-direct their play to other playmates, perhaps this would give us a glimpse into what I believe parents should be doing: listening to their children's desires, engaging with those who are different from one's norm, and learning that someone with less money can create their own fun, that the soda and chips that a child eats every now and then won't kill a child, that for the most part, adults and children can be trusted. I would argue that children understand equality better than adults; in their formative years they will often ask for a playdate with whoever treats them well. It is typically the parents who steer their children in one direction or another when it comes to class and race, as evidenced by participants. Granted, parents should always have the final say in their children's choice of playmates, given that safety is always a primary concern, but what are parents doing to teach their children through example that not everyone who is different from them is actually a bad person or "not like us"?

Allowing children to socialize and play with other children who eat "junk" food, who get disciplined differently from them, and who have parents who curse in the household could potentially lead children to question it and bring up the differences of household rules. In my own household, this offers us a chance to discuss what is acceptable in our household, usually resulting in an understanding that every family is different but it does not automatically make them better or worse. These situations give us an opportunity to discuss norms, income, and inequality on multiple levels, which I'm hoping will enable my children to be less judgmental as they age. I also acknowledge that when I do craft a playdate with PLUs I am actively doing so and understand the consequences of my actions. I am not having a playdate for the sake of my children *only*, although they may eventually benefit from this par-ticular social interaction.

This study gives us a small window into the world of the playdate, and how parents utilize it as a way to create community for themselves and their children. It also provides us with some insight into how to rethink how we manage our social worlds. How are we re-creating the very in-equalities that we encounter every day at work? Do we want our children to become the leaders of tomorrow with a narrow vision of how people live in the real world? These are all questions we should ask ourselves as we begin to determine whom our children can and cannot socialize with. Also, parents ought to be honest about the fact that, sometimes, they use other parents in order to gain access to the networks they desire for their own professional gain. The more we start to recognize what a playdate truly is, the more we can be honest with ourselves and our children. Finally, there can be only an appeal to understand that a playdate is really about parents' or teachers' desires and not necessarily the child's as a social being, since we have yet to document the true benefits of the playdate as an event that better integrates children with other children of all types. What is apparent, however, is that the playdate does socialize children among other children like them, thereby re-creating an exclusive elite class despite New York's economic, racial, and ethnic diversity.

NOTES

PREFACE

1 Tamara Mose Brown, *Raising Brooklyn: Nannies, Childcare, and Caribbeans Creating Community* (New York: New York University Press, 2011).

2 In gentrified Brooklyn public schools, the students come from a range of income levels and backgrounds.

3 Elijah Anderson, *Code of the Street: Decency, Violence, and Moral Life of the Inner City* (New York: Norton, 1999). Anderson further elaborates on what it means to be a "decent" black family versus a "street" family.

INTRODUCTION

1 Pierre Bourdieu, "The Forms of Capital," in *Handbook of Theory and Research for the Sociology of Education*, ed. John G. Richardson (New York: Greenwood, 1986), 241–58.

2 My previous ethnographic research on childcare providers included playdates formally, but playdates were not the unit of analysis. In my non-research life, I would say I informally noticed playdates as a phenomenon since I am a sociologist and now wired to look at social life differently.

3 Social capital was not gained by childcare providers in the same way that it was for parents.

4 Garrett Hardin, "The Tragedy of the Commons," *Science* 162 (1968): 1243–48; Harvey, "Future of the Commons," 101–7.

5 David Harvey, "The Future of the Commons," *Radical History Review* 109 (2011): 101.

6 Harvey, "Future of the Commons."

7 Robert D. Putnam, *Bowling Alone: The Collapse and Revival of American Community* (New York: Simon and Schuster, 2000).

8 Sharon Brookshaw, "The Material Culture of Children and Childhood: Understanding Childhood Objects in the Museum Context," *Journal of Material Culture* 14, no. 3 (2009): 365–83. Scholars of museum studies analyze how items are selected for display at various museums. See Brookshaw for more on this discipline.

9 Ibid. Commodification occurs because adults determine what "children's toys" are. These toys are typically store-bought, mass-produced, or handcrafted by an adult, instead of the toys that children actually make and play with. Displaying

child-made toys is not seen as sophisticated; therefore parents determine what is acceptable as a "toy."

10 Leslie Paris, *Children's Nature: The Rise of the American Summer Camp* (New York: New York University Press, 2008). A homogeneous setting among children to escape the heterogeneity of urban life has long been available at children's summer camps, where children of a certain class and consequently race could congregate outside the city. This has changed over time in camp settings, but this book will show how playdates revert to this homogeneous creation within New York City. Playdates are also constructed as play for the parents.

11 Ibid. Paris reflects on Rousseau and his theory of children being closer to nature.

12 Jean-Jacques Rousseau, *Emile, or On Education* (New York: Basic Books, 1979).

13 Markella Rutherford, *Adult Supervision Required: Private Freedom and Public Constraints for Parents and Children* (Piscataway, NJ: Rutgers University Press, 2011).

14 Viviana A. Zelizer, *Pricing the Priceless Child: The Changing Social Value of Children* (Princeton: Princeton University Press, 1985), 59.

15 Ibid., 97.

16 Alice S. Rossi, "A Biosocial Perspective on Parenting," *Daedalus* 106, no. 2 (1977): 25.

17 Peter N. Stearns, *Anxious Parents: A History of Modern Childrearing in America* (New York: New York University Press, 2004). See this text for more on the fears that influence how parents raise their children.

18 Adrianne Frech and Rachel T. Kimbro, "Maternal Mental Health, Neighborhood Characteristics, and Time Investments in Children," *Journal of Marriage and Family* 73, no. 3 (2011): 605–20.

19 Ibid., 606.

20 Allison James and Adrian L. James, "Childhood: Toward a Theory of Continuity and Change," *Annals of the American Academy of Political and Social Science* 575, no. 1 (2001): 25–37.

21 Holly Blackford, "Playground Panopticism: Ring-around-the-Children, a Pocketful of Women," *Childhood* 11, no. 2 (2004): 227–49; Arlie R. Hochschild, *The Managed Heart: Commercialization of Human Feeling* (Berkeley: University of California Press, 1983); Margaret Nelson, *Parenting Out of Control: Anxious Parents in Uncertain Times* (New York: New York University Press, 2010).

22 Blackford, "Playground Panopticism."

23 Michel Foucault, *Discipline and Punish: The Birth of the Prison* (New York: Pantheon, 1977).

24 Blackford, "Playground Panopticism."

25 Ibid.

26 Alison Pugh, *Longing and Belonging: Parents, Children, and Consumer Culture* (Berkeley: University of California Press, 2009).

27 Annette Lareau and Erin McNamara Horvat, "Moments of Social Inclusion and
    Exclusion: Race, Class, and Cultural Capital in Family-School Relationships,"
    Sociology of Education 72, no. 1 (1999): 37–53. See Alvin Rosenfeld and Nicole
    Wise, *The Over-Scheduled Child: Avoiding the Hyper-Parenting Trap* (New York:
    St. Martin's Griffin, 2001) for more about the possible negative effects of middle-
    class parenting strategies. Also see Lareau and Horvat for more on exclusion by
    race and class.

28 George Ritzer, "The McDonaldization of Society," *Journal of American Culture* 6,
    no. 1 (1983): 246.

29 Nelson, *Parenting Out of Control.*

30 Michele Lamont and Annette Lareau, "Cultural Capital: Allusions, Gaps and
    Glissandos in Recent Theoretical Developments," *Sociological Theory* 6, no. 2
    (1988): 153–68; Paul DiMaggio and John Mohr, "Cultural Capital, Educational
    Attainment, and Marital Selection," *American Journal of Sociology* 90, no. 6 (1985):
    1231–61; Alejandro Portes, "Social Capital: Its Origins and Applications in Modern
    Sociology," *Annual Review of Sociology* 24 (1998): 1–24.

31 Annette Lareau, *Unequal Childhoods: Class, Race, and Family Life* (Berkeley:
    University of California Press, 2003).

32 Portes, "Social Capital." Social chits are the conferred advantages stemming from
    the social capital and cultural capital gained through class membership. For
    example, if middle- to upper-middle-class parents have a network of professional
    friends or colleagues, the children of those parents can gain internships with the
    networks, thereby gaining a leg up in the professional world. Such favors lead to
    future mobility.

33 See 2010 census tract data in New York City for more detail.

34 John Hull Mollenkopf and Manuel Castells, eds., *Dual City: Restructuring New
    York* (New York: Russell Sage Foundation, 1992).

35 Department of City Planning, New York City, *The Newest New Yorkers:
    Characteristics of the City's Foreign-Born Population*, December 2013, 1, www.nyc.
    gov/html/dcp/pdf/census/nny2013/nny_2013.pdf.

36 Ibid., 3.

37 Moomah Café closed temporarily in 2012 and reopened under a similar name
    without the playdate feature, but still hosts birthday parties.

38 Mose Brown, *Raising Brooklyn.*

39 Gregory Smithsimon, *September 12: Community and Neighborhood Recovery at
    Ground Zero* (New York: New York University Press, 2011), 42–43. Smithsimon
    details these racialized images of crime in New York City. "White flight" refers to
    whites fleeing New York City for the suburbs as minorities entered the city for
    work and taking up residence.

40 Alex Vitale, *City of Disorder: How the Quality of Life Campaign Transformed New
    York Politics* (New York: New York University Press, 2008). See Vitale for more on

the effects of policing strategies used in New York City and how this has shaped New York's image.

41 George Gerbner and Larry Gross, "Living with Television: The Violence Profile," *Journal of Communication* 26, no. 2 (1976): 172–99. Cultivation theorists discuss the long-term effects of television and media consumption. The cultivation effect, then, is the cumulative effect of reality distortion as displayed in the media. Prototypical characteristics are the common traits of the victims. Typically the victim highlighted by the media is a young white girl who came from a loving family or a young child left unattended by a parent.

42 Seong Jae Min and John Feaster, "Missing Children in News: Racial and Gender Representation of Missing Children Cases in Television News" (paper presented at the Annual Meeting of the International Communication Association, Montreal, Quebec, May 21, 2008), http://citation.allacademic.com/meta/ p230591_index.html (accessed March 3, 2015).

43 Nelson, *Parenting Out of Control*. Nelson looks more deeply at how media influence professional middle-class parenting practices by their steady flood of images that promote societal violence or are highly sexualized.

CHAPTER 1. FROM PLAY TO PLAYDATE

1 Nelson, *Parenting Out of Control*. Also, this reminds one of the network television announcements such as "It's 10:00 p.m.; do you know where your children are?"—a great example of how television creates anxiety around child disappearance.

2 While "moral panic" was not the specific wording used by the participants in this book, they explicitly described concerns about how media influence the fear surrounding their own children's safety.

3 Ronald Burns and Charles Crawford, "School Shootings, the Media, and Public Fear: Ingredients for a Moral Panic," *Crime, Law and Social Change* 32 (1999): 147–68; Joel Best, *Random Violence: How We Talk about New Crimes and New Victims* (Berkeley: University of California Press, 1999).

4 Rutherford, *Adult Supervision Required*. In New York, the presence of children on the streets differs by neighborhood, depending on the class status associated with the neighborhood.

5 Jane Jacobs, *The Death and Life of Great American Cities* (New York: Vintage, 1961). Jacobs wrote this popular book to discuss how urban centers have been dismantled by urban planners.

6 C. C. Weiss, M. Purciel, M. Bader, J. W. Quinn, G. Lovasi, K. M. Neckerman, and A. G. Rundle, "Reconsidering Access: Park Facilities and Neighborhood Disamenities in New York City," *Journal of Urban Health* 88, no. 2 (2011): 297–310.

7 In New York City there are 959,122 households with kids. Of those, 521,386 are families with married couples; 344,755 are women-headed households. Women-headed families make up 36.2 percent of all families with kids in New York, more

than a third of the city's households (77,061 are men-headed households with kids). This leaves approximately 5,920 "nonfamily households" with kids under eighteen, which could possibly consist of parents who choose to have children without a partner. U.S. Census Bureau, "Family Structure, 2010 Census," prepared by Social Explorer, http://www.socialexplorer.com/tables/C2010/R10909270 (accessed March 13, 2015).

8 Georg Simmel, "The Stranger" (1908), in *Social Theory: The Multicultural and Classic Readings*, ed. Charles Lemert (Boulder: Westview, 1993), 199–204. According to Simmel, people can experience both closeness to and detachment from a community, if they are outsiders to the "native" group/community, yet are in continuous proximity to them.

9 Some may posit that we are discussing the theorist Ulrich Beck's concept of risk societies; however, Beck's discussion is more about living in an era in which technology creates risks beyond our control, but in which we have displaced responsibilities onto divisions of labor and systems that are so complex, no one individual can manage it. This is not the case for the moral panic perceived by parents.

10 Gill Valentine, "Images of Danger: Women's Sources of Information about the Spatial Distribution of Male Violence," *Area* 24, no. 1 (1992): 23.

11 Ibid. The private sphere of the home is considered a domestic space where the main occupants are family members. In this private sphere, women are able to control activities more closely.

12 New York City Police Department, "CompStat Report (NYPD)," http://www.nyc.gov/html/nypd/html/crime_prevention/crime_statistics.shtml (accessed January 23, 2012). There has been a sharp decrease in crime across all categories (murder, rape, robbery, assault, burglary, larceny) from 1990 to 2011. This would suggest that New York is in fact a much safer city to live in than it was two decades ago.

13 Pierre Bourdieu, *On Television* (New York: New Press, 1996).

14 Nelson, *Parenting Out of Control.*

15 Howard P. Chudacoff, *Children at Play: An American History* (New York: New York University Press, 2007).

16 According to Chudacoff, from the 1950s on, studies of children's deaths and injuries resulted in more rules for parents to follow. Now parents were faced with a long list of things to look out for: riding bikes, riding the schoolbus, wearing helmets, and so on.

17 Jean Baudrillard, *The Consumer Society: Myths and Structures* (London: Sage, 1998). Baudrillard provides more on simulacra or simulated copies of objects and mass-mediated "spectacles."

18 Rutherford, *Adult Supervision Required.*

19 Sinikka Elliott and Elyshia Aseltine, "Raising Teenagers in Hostile Environments: How Race, Class, and Gender Matter for Mothers' Protective Carework," *Journal of Family Issues* 34, no. 6 (2013): 1–26. In this article, an intersectionality approach

details how mothers read danger in their children's communities and what strategies are used to combat parental fears.

CHAPTER 2. MY PLACE OR YOURS?

1   Some public parks in New York City have park personnel who gather used children's toys that are taken out each day for children to play with, and are later stored in the park facilities at the playground.

2   Richard D. Ashmore, Frances K. Del Boca, and Arthur J. Wohlers, "Gender Stereotypes," in *The Social Psychology of Female-Male Relations*, ed. R. D. Ashmore and F. K. Del Boca (Orlando, FL: Academic Press, 1986), 69–119; Kay Deaux, "Sex and Gender," *Annual Review of Psychology* 36 (1985): 49–81; David L. Hamilton, *Cognitive Processes in Stereotyping and Intergroup Behavior* (Hillsdale, NJ: Lawrence Erlbaum, 1981); Margaret Mooney Marini and Mary C. Brinton, "Sex Typing in Occupational Socialization," in *Sex Segregation in the Workplace: Trends, Explanations, Remedies*, ed. B. Reskin (Washington, D.C.: National Academy Press, 1984), 192–232.

3   Victoria E. Bynum, *Unruly Women* (Chapel Hill: University of North Carolina Press, 1992); Nancy Duncan, "Renegotiating Gender and Sexuality in Public and Private Spaces," in *BodySpace: Destabilizing Geographies of Gender and Sexuality*, ed. Nancy Duncan (New York: Routledge, 1996); Adrienne Rich, *Of Woman Born* (New York: Norton, 1996); Gill Valentine, "The Geography of Women's Fear," *Area* 21 (1989): 385–390.

4   J. H. Hyde, "How Large Are Cognitive Gender Differences?" *American Psychologist* 36 (1981): 892–901; Eleanor Emmons Maccoby and Carol Nagy Jacklin, *The Psychology of Sex Differences* (Stanford: Stanford University Press, 1974); R. Plomin and T. T. Foch, "Sex Differences and Individual Differences," *Child Development* 52 (1981): 383–85; Peggy R. Sanday, "Female Status in the Public Domain," in *Woman, Culture, and Society*, ed. Michelle Z. Rosaldo and Louise Lamphere (Stanford: Stanford University Press, 1974).

5   Erving Goffman, *The Presentation of Self in Everyday Life* (New York: Anchor, 1959).

6   Rohan's teacher was a private school teacher from Manhattan who now freelances for such cooperatives, where parents want to organize their own preschool experience in the home.

7   Mose Brown, *Raising Brooklyn*.

8   Parents admitted to setting up private play in their homes after only one or two meetings. They are having playdates with parents who seem familiar because of the school setting, yet they do not really know the person, which contradicts the very fears parents expressed about New York.

9   I found the marker "very Caucasian" to mean that Elizabeth was conscious of her place on Long Island as a white woman who perhaps sees her world mainly through that lens.

10 These cooperatives are the exchange of free babysitting, but once again, class is invoked. Participants understood this arrangement to mean an organized childcare system by upper-class parents.

11 Mose Brown, *Raising Brooklyn.*

12 An "ended group" means a group that is not seeking new members. They are an established group with similar interests that have been decided on by the parents.

13 Since these are online businesses, there was no way to determine where the majority of their customers for this item are located. See Familystickers.com for examples of playdate business cards or Etsy's Print Your Party webpage.

14 None of the participants in my study said that they used these business cards.

15 Joyce L. Epstein, "After the Bus Arrives: Resegregation in Desegregated Schools," *Journal of Social Issues* 41, no. 3 (1985): 23–43. Epstein surveys literature on the impact of busing on integration and social outcomes.

16 Carmen's daughter has darker skin than the friend she was playing with and therefore referred to "white" as the color of his skin as compared to hers since she is nonwhite.

CHAPTER 3. WHO IS IN AND WHO IS OUT?

1 Annette Lareau, "Social Class Differences in Family-School Relationships: The Importance of Cultural Capital," *Sociology of Education* 60 (April 1987): 73–85; Lamont and Lareau, "Cultural Capital."

2 Lareau, *Unequal Childhoods.*

3 Mose Brown, *Raising Brooklyn.* The book features a lengthier discussion and history of the class and gentrification dynamics between residents in Carroll Gardens.

4 Annette Lareau, "Invisible Inequality: Social Class and Childrearing in Black Families and White Families," *American Sociological Review* 67, no. 5 (2002): 747–76.

5 Annette Lareau, *Home Advantage: Social Class and Parental Involvement in Elementary Education* (London: Falmer, 1989).

6 Lareau and Horvat, "Moments of Social Inclusion and Exclusion."

7 Park Slope has million- to multimillion-dollar brownstone row houses that run adjacent to one of Brooklyn's largest parks, Prospect Park. The area is sought out by many families (gentrifiers) since it is located near a variety of hip restaurants, boutique shopping, public transportation, and well-funded schools. A Park Slopian would be considered wealthy, white, and liberal.

8 Ralph B. McNeal, "Parental Involvement as Social Capital: Differential Effectiveness on Science Achievement, Truancy, and Dropping Out," *Social Forces* 78, no. 1 (1999): 117–44.

9 See Goffman, *Presentation of Self,* for a more elaborate definition.

10 Nelson, *Parenting Out of Control.* Nelson found similar results with the professional middle-class parents. In her book, parents sought educational and

extracurricular activities to secure social and cultural capital gains for their child's future. The anxiety stems from living in an insecure economic climate that is not only local, but global.

11 Jonathan J. Brower, "The Professionalization of Organized Youth Sport: Social Psychological Impacts and Outcomes," *Annals of the American Academy of Political and Social Science* 445, no. 1 (1979): 39–46; Joseph L. Mahoney, Angel L. Harris, and Jacquelynne S. Eccles, "Organized Activity Participation, Positive Youth Development, and the Over-Scheduling Hypothesis," *Social Policy Report* 20, no. 4 (2006).

12 See Joseph L. Mahoney, Angel L. Harris, and Jacquelynne S. Eccles, "The Over-Scheduling Myth" (Research to Results, no. 12, Child Trends, Washington, D.C., 2008).

13 This book defines a playdate as an arranged meeting, organized by parents or caregivers, between two or more children in order to play together at a specific time and place, not necessarily to promote academic skills.

14 See Carmen's discussion of needing a break or mommy time in chapter 2.

15 Lareau, *Unequal Childhoods*. See this book for more about how material conditions created a varied learning environment and exchange with adults and other children.

16 For more discussion and links to statewide data, see "New York's Common Core Test Scores," editorial, *New York Times*, August 7, 2013, http://www.nytimes.com/2013/08/08/opinion/new-yorks-common-core-test-scores.html?_r=0 (accessed May 20, 2015).

17 For the latest standards, see the Department of Education website for New York City.

18 See Lareau, *Unequal Childhoods*, for more on the topic of social and cultural capital being acquired not merely through parental influence, but by schools that are run by those of middle-class backgrounds.

19 Ibid.

20 Ibid., 97.

21 Oneka LaBennett, *She's Mad Real: Popular Culture and West Indian Girls in Brooklyn* (New York: New York University Press, 2011). LaBennett provides an extensive review of the negative views of poor people's consumption patterns.

22 See Census Bureau data for income and wealth figures by race.

23 Eduardo Bonilla-Silva, "From Bi-Racial to Tri-Racial: Towards a New System of Racial Stratification in the USA," *Ethnic and Racial Studies* 27, no. 6 (2004): 931–50.

24 Ibid.

25 Lareau, *Unequal Childhoods*, 247.

26 Ibid., 3.

27 Brookshaw, "Material Culture of Children," 365–83.

28 New York City's public school system reinforces competition by making musical auditions a requirement to get into some of the more highly regarded middle and high schools.

29 Mose Brown, *Raising Brooklyn*.

30 Mildred Parten, "Social Participation among Pre-School Children," *Journal of Abnormal and Social Psychology* 27, no. 3 (1932): 243–69.

31 Mose Brown, *Raising Brooklyn*. The book provides more about the household hierarchy and how nannies use public spaces to counteract the pressures of the private sphere.

32 Ibid. This book offers more on how nannies viewed having employers structure their day at work.

CHAPTER 4. PLAYDATE ETIQUETTE

1 Marjorie Devault, *Feeding the Family: The Social Organization of Caring as Gendered Work* (Chicago: University of Chicago Press, 1991); Elaine Bell Kaplan, "Food as a Metaphor for Care: Middle-School Kids Talk about Family, School, and Class Relationships," *Journal of Contemporary Ethnography* 29, no. 4 (2000): 474–509.

2 Mose Brown, *Raising Brooklyn*; Mose Brown, "Who's the Boss? The Political Economy of Unpaid Care Work and Food Sharing in Brooklyn USA," *Feminist Economics* 18, no. 3 (2012): 1–24.

3 Devault, *Feeding the Family*.

4 Kaplan, "Food as a Metaphor for Care."

5 Erving Goffman, *Interaction Ritual: Essays on Face-to-Face Interaction* (Chicago: Aldine, 1967).

6 Goffman, *Presentation of Self*.

7 Mose Brown, *Raising Brooklyn*. The book provides more on foodways. Foodways are the social and cultural practices of food consumption and preparation. In this study, foodways varied according to social class.

8 For an in-depth discussion of Pirate's Booty and its calorie and fat content as well as how it is marketed as a healthy alternative, see William Grimes, "The Aisle Less Traveled: A Stranger in a Junk Food World," *New York Times*, March 27, 2002.

9 Jonathan L. Biltstein and W. Douglas Evans, "Use of Nutrition Facts Panels among Adults Who Make Household Food Purchasing Decisions," *Journal of Nutrition Education and Behavior* 38, no. 6 (2006): 360–64. Biltstein and Evans write about nutritional literacy and beliefs in their quantitative analysis of 1,139 adults who make food purchasing decisions in the household. They found that more educated females and those who were married looked at nutrition fact labels more frequently than others.

10 It should be noted here that pizza is not necessarily considered a healthy snack, but depending on whether it is baked at home or at a restaurant, it may have

nutritional value. The spectrum of opinions on the nutritional value of pizza was vast in this study.

11 Mose Brown, *Raising Brooklyn*. See the book for more on social food space as a de-commodification of food representation.

12 Devault, *Feeding the Family*.

13 Pugh, *Longing and Belonging*. Pugh discusses the deeper choices that parents and children make based on institutional systems of inequality.

14 Nannies often admitted to using corporal punishment with their own children, but did not use it with the children they cared for. Nor in my four years of fieldwork with them did I see a childcare provider use excessive force or spanking with a child.

15 Kirby Deater-Deckard and Sandra Scarr, "Parenting Stress among Dual-Earner Mothers and Fathers: Are There Gender Differences?," *Journal of Family Psychology* 10, no. 1 (1994): 45–59; Marjorie E. Starrels, "Gender Differences in Parent-Child Relations," *Journal of Family Issues* 15, no. 1 (1994): 148–65. Both articles explore gender differences in disciplining children.

16 Franco had taken child development courses and received a certificate in child development and therefore felt qualified in his decisions about discipline.

17 It is unclear whether Franco's method is seen as model behavior with positive outcomes for other children or simply obnoxious behavior for the other parent involved.

CHAPTER 5. THE BIRTHDAY PARTY

1 For an even more pronounced sense of how birthday parties have become commodified, view episodes of the reality television show *Outrageous Kid Parties* on TLC on the Discovery Network, where parents invite hundreds of guests, take their child across the country as their gift, and organize parties that include DJs, visual props, entertainers, food trucks, simulation rides, large detailed cakes, water slides, famous guests and lavish costumes. Parents spend upwards of $20,000 on a ten-year-old's birthday party.

2 As upper-middle-class children age into grades 2 to 4, the activities, as recalled by participants, included ice skating, indoor rock climbing, pool parties in the suburbs of the city, and party buses (a large limousine bus with disco lights and music). According to the economist Robert H. Frank, an "expenditure cascade" occurs when upper-middle-class consumers spend increasing amounts on an item, causing their peers to do the same. Robert H. Frank, Adam S. Levine, and Oege Dijk, "Expenditure Cascades" (paper presented at American Economic Association, 2010), SSRN eLibrary, http://ssrm.com/paer=1690612.

3 Most birthday parties tend to be held on the weekends. Some do happen after school hours as well.

4 Alison J. Clarke, "Making Sameness: Mothering, Commerce and the Culture of Children's Birthday Parties," in *Gender and Consumption*, ed. Emma Casey and Lydia Martens (Aldershot, England: Ashgate, 2007), 79–96.

5 Ibid.

6 Class judgments determined what is acceptable food. What is missing from this statement is that perhaps the middle- to upper-middle-class mom has more time to dictate her own schedule and cook vegan cupcakes, whereas the working-class parents may need to order something quickly and are not able to spend time on such domestic labor.

7 *Jamie Oliver's Food Revolution* aired on ABC and showed one chef's attempt to combat the obesity issue around the United States by targeting public school lunches served in cafeterias. He attempted to show how schools could integrate healthier foods without compromising taste.

8 Fathers were typically present at birthday parties since they mostly occur on the weekends. During the weekdays, fathers tended to be working; mothers would state in their interviews that the dad would be sent to birthday parties on the weekends with the kids in order to spend time with the children. Mothers who worked outside the home tended to be at home for more hours with the kids during the workday than fathers.

9 This hyper-playdate can be seen as a hyper-enclosed commons. Parents are able to network in the same way they would through the playdate in someone's home. In the birthday party scenario, there are more people to potentially network with in this enclosed, private space.

10 See the Party Wagon blog at http://party-wagon.com/party-packages/, where $85 buys you the theme of the party, or a custom party for six to eight children costs $2,500, not including additional guests, which cost $50 additional per person. There are several websites offering such services and even more ideas on social media such as Pinterest.

11 By "playground-worthy," I mean worthy of discussing on the playground the following week. This worthiness is completely subjective.

CONCLUSION

1 See Jane Jacobs, *The Death and Life of Great American Cities*, reissue edition (New York: Vintage, 1992) for more on how public space is theorized as a democratic space and how living in the same neighborhood could contribute to the elimination of poverty. Also see Elijah Anderson, *Cosmopolitan Canopy: Race and Civility in Everyday Life* (reprint, New York: Norton, 2012) and his discussion of shared public space and the creation of a forced society where resources are shared. Douglas S. Massey and Nancy A. Denton, in *American Apartheid: Segregation and the Making of the Underclass* (Cambridge: Harvard University Press, 1993), also discuss how shared physical space does not create equality, but rather results in conflict over resources.

INDEX

ABOUT THE AUTHOR

Tamara R. Mose is Associate Professor of Sociology at Brooklyn College, City University of New York. She is the author of *Raising Brooklyn: Nannies, Childcare, and Caribbeans Creating Community*, also from New York University Press.